Better Homes and Gardens®

YOUR BEDROOMS

BETTER HOMES AND GARDENS® BOOKS

Editor: Gerald M. Knox
Art Director: Ernest Shelton
Managing Editor: David A. Kirchner

Associate Art Directors: Linda Ford Vermie, Neoma Alt West,
Randall Yontz
Copy and Production Editors: Marsha Jahns,
Mary Helen Schiltz, Carl Voss, David A. Walsh
Assistant Art Directors: Harijs Priekulis, Tom Wegner
Senior Graphic Designers: Alisann Dixon, Lynda Haupert,
Lyne Neymeyer
Graphic Designers: Mike Burns, Mike Eagleton, Deb Miner,
Stan Sams, D. Greg Thompson, Darla Whipple, Paul Zimmerman

Vice President, Editorial Director: Doris Eby
Group Editorial Services Director: Duane L. Gregg

General Manager: Fred Stines
Director of Publishing: Robert B. Nelson
Vice President, Director of Retail Marketing: Jamie Martin
Vice President, Director of Direct Marketing: Arthur Heydendael

All About Your House: Your Bedrooms

Project Editor: James A. Hufnagel
Associate Editor: Willa Rosenblatt Speiser
Assistant Editor: Leonore A. Levy
Copy and Production Editors: Nancy Nowiszewski, Carl Voss
Building and Remodeling Editor: Joan McCloskey
Furnishings and Design Editor: Shirley Van Zante
Garden Editor: Douglas A. Jimerson
Money Management and Features Editor: Margaret Daly

Associate Art Director: Randall Yontz
Graphic Designer: D. Greg Thompson
Electronic Text Processor: Sally Schomers
Contributing Editors: Jill Abeloe Mead, Stephen Mead
Contributing Senior Writer: Paul Kitzke
Contributors: Karol Brookhouser, Denise L. Caringer,
Debbie Felton, Cathy Howard, Jean LemMon, Peter Stephano

Special thanks to William N. Hopkins, Babs Klein, and
Don Wipperman for their valuable contributions to this book.

INTRODUCTION

To sleep: perchance to dream..." wrote William Shakespeare. The pages that follow delve into the spaces we sleep in, and tell how to turn any dreams you might have about your bedrooms into reality.

Like a good night's sleep, a good bedroom begins with a comfortable bed. *Your Bedrooms* says a lot about beds. Here you'll learn how to select a mattress and bedding, where to locate beds, how to custom-build them, and ways that alternatives to the traditional bed—such as bunks, trundles, Murphys, and sleeping lofts—can solve bedroom space problems.

But the best bedrooms are more than just places to lay your head. For a child, a bedroom is a special environment where Peter Pan or Kermit the Frog might visit. For grown-ups, bedrooms can and should be equally inviting as places to sink into a late night movie or an engrossing mystery, catch up on correspondence, enjoy a quiet chat, or express intimacy.

A bedroom is more personal than any other room in your house. The way one is planned, how it's styled and colored, the coverings on beds and windows, accessories and amenities, all contribute to the difference between a bedroom you look forward to curling up in and one that's just ho-hum.

Your Bedrooms devotes more than 100 color photographs, plans, and illustrations to ideas and information you can use to better the bedrooms at your house. If you enjoy this book, you may be interested in seeing other volumes in the Better Homes & Gardens® ALL ABOUT YOUR HOUSE Library. This wide-ranging encyclopedia of home decorating, improvement, planning, and management covers just about every area and aspect of a modern-day house.

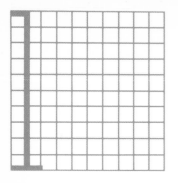

EVALUATING THE BEDROOMS AT YOUR HOUSE

Are you happy with the bedrooms at your house as sleeping spaces? Would you like them to provide more storage, more living space, more color? Use this chapter to help analyze your bedrooms' potential, their appearance, and how well they function. Later chapters tell how to plan and implement changes, select decorative accessories, add amenities, and plot strategies for making sleeping spaces as attractive and practical as they can be.

FIRST, ARE YOUR BEDROOMS LARGE ENOUGH?

All too often, bedrooms are among the most cramped spaces in a home. In some cases, the master bedroom may be spacious, but one or more of the secondary bedrooms have barely adequate dimensions; in another home, no bedroom seems to have quite enough room. If you have such a situation at your house, take heart. With careful planning and creative use of space, just about any room big enough to accommodate a bed can become a pleasant place to lay your head.

Even a twin bed is a good-size piece of furniture, and any bed meant to sleep two people is a massive item. Of course beds come in different sizes, but for anyone larger than an infant, you probably wouldn't want a mattress smaller than twin size. With larger beds, your choice of double, queen, or king sizes will make a big difference in how much space the bed occupies. Templates on pages 156 and 157 let you experiment with bed sizes and furniture arrangements.

Should you emphasize your bed?

Once you've decided what size bed will work best for you, your next furnishings decision is how prominent you want it to be. If your bed is unusually attractive—like the charming antique pine bed shown *opposite*—or you have a large house and really don't need your bedroom for much besides sleeping, highlighting the bed may be the best decorating choice to make. In that case, aesthetics is the main concern; Chapter 2—"Style & Color"—provides an abundance of decorating ideas. If you want to call even more attention to a bed, see Chapter 7—"Sewing for the Bedroom"—for eye-catching ways to dress it up.

Yet another way to play up a bed is with a creative furniture arrangement. For example, just angling the bed out from a corner, as shown here, turns the bed into a star attraction and could free space in unexpected places. Or consider floating your bed in the center of the room, perhaps with a convenient storage unit serving as the headboard.

Redecorate to stretch bedroom space

To gain space visually as well as literally, look around and see where you can pare down furnishings and accessories. For example, the occupants of the bedroom pictured *opposite* gained inches of usable space by skipping a bulky window treatment. Here, a stained-glass window panel provides privacy as well as charm.

Eliminating a bed frame and using a space-saving platform bed instead also will bring a little extra space into active use. In addition, a platform bed can help you reduce standard bedroom storage furniture because clothing and bedding can go into drawers beneath the platform. Or there may be a dramatic way to increase bedroom space that stops short of adding on. Chapter 5—"Alternative Sleeping Strategies"— presents a variety of solutions to space problems.

EVALUATING THE BEDROOMS AT YOUR HOUSE

WHAT MORE CAN YOUR BEDROOMS DO?

It seems a shame to have good-looking rooms that are used only when you're asleep. If that's the case at your house, think about adding a few extras, such as seating for two or more, a desk large enough to work at, good lighting, bookshelves, or an entertainment center. These practical amenities can make the difference between a room that's underused and one that leads as full a life as you do.

The blue-white-and-natural-wood room pictured *at right* is average in size, but extras make it special. A fireplace, sofa, occasional table, and wicker accessories all add up to a livable bedroom that welcomes its occupants at all times of day.

Just one comfortable chair in a bedroom makes it a cozy spot to relax in. If you have a little more floor space, add another chair to create a conversation area. If you study all the angles, there probably are several more nice touches your bedroom could offer.

A window with a view, a wood-burning stove, a fireplace—any of these can turn a stay-at-home bedroom into the kind of hideaway a country inn's guests might envy. A bedroom with a few square feet to spare can earn its keep as a daytime home office. And a guest room that's used only a few times a year can lead an active second life as a family room or den. Chapter 8—"Amenities"—tells how to make the most of all the appealing architectural features your bedrooms may have, and how to add touches that make a room special.

Do you have visions of an adult suite, complete with spa, dressing room, and entertainment center? Or do you want to turn a children's bedroom into a daytime playroom? Chapters 3 and 4—"Planning a Master Bedroom" and "Planning Other Bedrooms"—give practical advice, imaginative inspiration, and floor plans of successful projects much like the ones you may be hoping to embark upon.

EVALUATING THE BEDROOMS AT YOUR HOUSE

DO YOUR CHILDREN HAVE THEIR OWN ROOMS?

More than other bedrooms, children's rooms have to be programmed for change. The room you set up years ago for a truck-collecting toddler may be enclosed by the same four walls as the one your twelve-year-old soccer player comes home to now, but it probably looks very different. Some things don't change, however. Having a place of his or her own gives a child a sense of identity and importance, as well as a place to sleep and keep things. When space is limited, it isn't always possible to provide a separate room for each child, but there are lots of ways you can divide rooms and arrange sleeping areas to maximize activity space and privacy. This will help you ensure that the area is as special to the child as the child is to you.

One of the best ways to help children feel they "belong" is to give them a place that reflects their interests. The brightly colored car-design sheets and wallpaper border in the bedroom pictured *at right* make it clear where this boy's heart is. They also make a statement about whose room it is.

The room shown here may reflect its occupant's interests, but there's a lot of grown-up handiwork in it. The bedskirt, duvet cover, and matching wallpaper border treatment were products of Mom's imagination. To learn about making skirts and duvet covers, see pages 106-113.

If you aren't sure you're using the space in a child's bedroom to best advantage, turn to Chapter 4—"Planning Other Bedrooms"—for pointers. If space is very limited, planning how to use it becomes especially important. Pages 70-73 and 78 and 79 show how snug spaces were turned into very special quarters for children.

When you allocate space and choose furnishings for young children, look ahead to the transition from play to study. Think about where a desk will go, whether a crib corner is big enough for a bed, and where bookshelves can go when toy chests are discarded. Try to plan storage that can expand as a child's possessions multiply in quantity and size.

The inset photo *opposite* shows how storage units tucked under a mini sleeping loft provide accessible, abundant storage. For an older child, this niche could, with minor changes, become a study center.

EVALUATING THE BEDROOMS AT YOUR HOUSE

WHAT LOOK DO YOU WANT FOR YOUR BEDROOMS?

Even more than public rooms such as kitchens and living rooms, your home's bedrooms can express your family's uniqueness and personality. But because bedrooms are not on display, they're often neglected as decorating opportunities. Color, style, furniture arrangement, and accessories are just some of the tools you can use to help your bedroom decorating schemes come alive. Once you know what look you want, you'll be well on your way to achieving it.

Whether you want a bedroom that's snug and country-cozy or spacious and elegant, the right combination of colors, patterns, furniture, and accessories is the key. For example, in the bedroom pictured *at left,* an antique sleigh bed and rich rust-colored walls work unexpectedly well with the bold pattern of a geometric rug, while contemporary apothecary lamps and wall graphics contrast pleasingly with a vintage marble-topped nightstand. The result of this juxtaposition and variety: an intimate mood and eclectic decorating style that's just what the owners wanted. To help you get started in the direction your tastes want to take you, turn to pages 20-37.

You may be sure of the colors and styles you like but still be in a quandary about how to create a masterful master bedroom. If that's one of your decorating goals, you'll find a variety of ideas and suggestions in Chapter 3—"Planning a Master Bedroom." Chapter 4 includes the equivalent for other bedrooms.

No matter what your design recipe, details are important. A custom coverlet or coordinated pillows and window treatment may be what it takes to set your room apart. Chapter 7 gives step-by-step instructions for sewing pillow shams, comforter covers, quilts, and many other distinctive projects.

Another way to give a bedroom a look all its—and your—own is to build a bed for it. Chapter 9—"Bedroom Projects You Can Build"—tells how to construct a variety of intriguing beds, including a platform bed, bunk bed, and water bed frame.

DO YOU HAVE SPACE FOR OVERNIGHT GUESTS?

When overnight guests are expected, do you get insomnia just thinking about finding a place to put them? Space for visitors runs the gamut from a full-fledged guest room to a pull-down bed-in-the-wall. What category your guest accommodations fall into depends on the space you're working with and how often you have sleepover company.

The well-upholstered den shown *at right* is a perfect spot for reading, relaxing, and getting away from it all. Family members use it regularly. It's also an almost-instant guest room, convertible to sleeping quarters on a moment's notice.

Standard twin-size box springs rest directly on the floor. Throw pillows provide enough back support to make each bed work like a sofa for daytime use. But the "upholstery" on each really is a fitted sheet. Fresh sheets, blankets, and pillows—stored in a handy closet—are all that's needed to turn the room into sleeping space. For information about mattresses, linens, and other items for any bedroom, see Chapter 10—"Choosing and Buying Bedroom Furnishings."

If you often have overnight guests, a guest room as complete as this one is a great convenience and doesn't take as much extra room as you might think. For more about setting up welcoming guest quarters in double-duty rooms, see pages 130 and 131.

If overnight visitors are more the exception than the rule at your house, chances are you can make do with a sleep sofa in the family room or a Murphy bed in just about any room in the house.

Do your youngsters like to have friends sleep over? To accommodate these special guests, you can use space even more imaginatively than for adults. For example, a hideaway bunk bed or loft/play space like those on pages 76-79 can delight the child in residence and also provide cozy sleeping space for overnight visitors. And if you'd like to build a bunk bed for your children's guests, see pages 138 and 139.

EVALUATING THE BEDROOMS AT YOUR HOUSE

CAN YOU STRETCH BEDROOM SPACE?

No matter how much space you have, it eventually gets filled. And once it's filled, it never seems large enough. There's always one more piece of furniture, one more function to be added. A room with too much furniture in it looks crowded and inefficient. Sometimes rearranging the furniture in creative new ways opens up space. Sometimes more drastic action is called for. Then you may have to consider moving a wall, cutting down a wall to partial height, or knocking one down entirely and borrowing space from an adjoining room.

The most dramatic solution to space problems is to physically add more space. This may mean annexing the room next door, turning a closet into a dressing room, or bumping out with an addition. Maybe you can provide direct access to a nearby bath and create a master suite. In Chapter 6—"Bedroom Building Basics"—you'll find advice and illustrations about removing walls, putting up new walls, installing a vanity, and adding other features.

If you think a somewhat less radical approach will work, turn your attention to furniture arranging. Chapters 3 and 4 will guide you in planning your bedroom spaces, and the handy templates on pages 156 and 157 will let you try out countless arrangements with nary a strained muscle or scratched floor.

Dual-purpose furniture and super-efficient storage will help you make the most of your space. The reading room/ bedroom pictured *at left* shows how shallow ceiling-high bookshelves can minimize clutter by storing books and collectibles. The wicker basket, too, provides both storage and decorative flair, yet takes up very little floor space.

Another way to expand space is through visual trickery. For example, rooms will appear larger if you use light colors on walls and on large pieces of furniture. Mirrors, strategically placed, will double visual space, and unencumbered windows will help, too. For more about decorative techniques that will help you make the most of any bedroom, see Chapter 2.

DO YOU HAVE ENOUGH STORAGE IN YOUR BEDROOMS?

Finding enough storage space is a constant struggle in almost every room of almost every home. In bedrooms, the storage crisis is likely to become acute. You need hanging space, drawer or built-in cabinet space, counter space, shelf space—all in what are often among the smallest rooms of the house. As always, careful evaluation and good planning are essential.

The first step to improving the storage in your bedrooms is to take inventory of what must be stored.

Certainly clothes occupy a large portion of storage space in most bedrooms. But some clothes are off-season items that could be stored outside the bedroom until the weather changes. Then you only need to provide hanging and drawer space for in-season clothes. Analyze, too, what types of clothes you have the most of. If a majority are foldable, perhaps you can add drawer or shelf space in your closet, rather than sacrifice valuable floor space to dressers.

In addition to clothes, you may need storage space for grooming aids, or extra bedding and bath linens. And if your bedrooms accommodate extra functions such as hobbies, TV watching, or reading, you probably need specialized storage for these activities. The bedroom pictured *at left* and *above* takes diverse needs into account and approaches the storage question from the ground up. Books and magazines are fitted neatly into open shelves adjacent to the bed, and drawers under the bed's platform store linens and sleepwear. Pillows are banked against the angled headboard; its slanted front opens, as shown in the close-up, to provide space for extra bedding. You'll find more about storage for adult bedrooms on pages 46 and 47.

In children's rooms, storage needs are more diverse. Toys, books, study aids, and treasures ranging from dollhouses to birds' nests are just some of the myriad items that find their way into children's rooms. In addition to small-scale versions of the suggestions illustrated on this page, child-height shelf space, easy-sliding drawers, and bins that hold nearly everything are a few possibilities. Pages 60 and 61 can help you maximize storage in children's bedrooms.

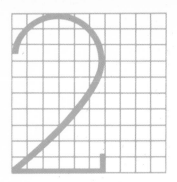

STYLE & COLOR

Just because bedrooms are for sleeping doesn't mean their decorating style has to put you to sleep. A bedroom should be restful, private, and comfortable—but not dull. Start with a basic space, add some eye-pleasing furnishings in colors you're comfortable with, and your bedroom is on its way to becoming a welcome retreat. Whether you're starting from scratch or using furniture you've had for years, here are suggestions for making the pieces work together.

You probably already know whether you prefer a look that's traditional, contemporary, or somewhere in between. That's good, but don't let style labels keep you from experimenting or using colors and furnishings you like.

If you're drawn to traditional styling but aren't sure that you want soft colors and dainty prints, there are other ways to achieve the look you like—and a change of pace at the same time. If solids or larger scale patterns will work in your room, use them; the end result likely will be intriguing.

The inviting room pictured *at right* owes much of its charm to an interesting mix of periods and an unexpected touch of color and contemporary details. The beautifully carved four-poster bed says "traditional," but instead of an elaborate window treatment, modern mini-slat blinds, softened with white sheer draperies, filter light and provide privacy. Forest-green walls create an inviting, denlike coziness. On the bed, contemporary plaid linens add an unexpectedly tailored touch, and a modern-day comforter in a red-and-green plaid provides warm color contrast with traditional flair.

To add interest to any traditional scheme, consider a mix of pieces instead of a carefully matched "suite." This room gains warmth and personality from a combination of antiques and secondhand finds: two very unmatching rugs, an old landscape painting and a still life, a Victorian chaise longue (visible at left), and a cane-seated wooden armchair. Color pulls the furnishings together: The rugs share red hues and the chaise is upholstered to match the walls.

CASUAL

Do you like to sprawl on the bed to watch television, read, or listen to music? Do you occasionally enjoy a meal or snack in your bedroom? If so, then a casual decorating scheme is just right for you. Although casual styling is easy to live with, it takes as much planning as any other style does. Here are some pointers for designing a casual bedroom that's as attractive and pulled-together as it is comfortable.

Appealing, no-fuss furnishings in a carefree blend of styles and colors are the keys to a successful casual room. To create a pleasantly cohesive room that combines relaxed, unstudied comfort with efficient function, you need to keep a few basics in mind. Color, textures, and a shared informal quality can help to unite a furnishings mix.

The bedroom shown *at right,* with its wipe-clean breakfast table, extra pillows, and cheerful morning sunlight, invites comfortable lounging and combines convenience with charm. More nice touches: graceful, well-placed reading lamps, simple paper window shades, and painted wood bed and side chair.

A relaxed yet crisply contrasting blue-and-white color scheme holds things together. The checked design on the apothecary jars echoes the bold pattern on the quilt, but to avoid a rigidly matched effect, the blue-and-white accent pillows offer a variety of patterns and textures.

Informal rooms may vary in style from country to contemporary, but they share certain features. Among those are:
• *Comfort.* Your furnishings should be pleasing to the touch, welcoming to the body, and attractive to the eye.
• *Convenience.* Before you buy an item, ask yourself if it will be easy to live with.
• *Easy-care materials.* It's hard to put on formal airs when you're surrounded with durable, easy-care materials, whether they're natural or manufactured. Think in terms of polyurethaned wood or frankly plastic plastic; cotton, wool, or durable synthetic-blend upholstery (all fabrics usually treated to resist stains); and undemanding greenery or no-care collectibles.

ECLECTIC

Eclectic rooms are basically mix-and-match projects—experiments in contrasting, blending, borrowing, and even building. In an eclectic bedroom you can place a treasured pine country armoire next to a favorite contemporary lounge chair, or spark a standard 1950s bedroom with unexpected out-of-period accents. Whatever your preference, the key to successful eclectic schemes is to keep the mood balanced. An old piece and a new piece are more likely to look good together if they're both formal or informal, and both country in feeling or factory-built and up-to-date for their times.

Like the casual schemes we've already discussed, eclecticism isn't a matter of haphazardly tossing together a catchall collection of pieces. Instead, it calls for a sophisticated design sense and the confidence to deliberately and authoritatively mix the best from different times and places.

The advantage of adopting an eclectic approach is the freedom it affords you to create the most personalized home possible. The result is often a delightfully unpredictable mix that's always interesting to live with. You may find that you see classic pieces in a new way when you mix them with items from other periods. A Queen Anne writing table and chair, for instance, can take on newfound excitement when placed against stark white walls and accented with modern bed sheets and artwork.

To create your own pleasing mix, look for pieces that are well-designed and tasteful, and that share a common mood. An old quilt can be right at home with casual modern chairs, but it may look out of place with a curvaceous Art Deco dressing table or a formal Chippendale armchair. Similarly, a favorite braided rug that blends in easily with a casual country or contemporary setting probably will not work in a formal room.

Look at the bedroom shown *at right* to see how various decorating styles work together. Several types of furnishings are used: a skirted table, a wicker chair and ottoman, a Chinese rug, and modern artwork. Not only do the furnishings share a color scheme—white and related tints of blue and purple—but each item also is softly informal in mood.

COUNTRY

Country means soft colors, flowery prints, glowing, polished wood, natural-fiber fabrics, flourishing plants, and most of all, a mood that's warm, homey, relaxing, and inviting. Country bedrooms owe much of their charm to the varied textures and colors of their furnishings and accessories, from braided rugs and chintz armchairs to fresh flowers, dried herbs, and hand-glazed pottery. And many country-look items—hand-stitched quilts and pine night tables, for example—go especially well in bedrooms because that's where they were meant to be used.

The crowning glory of the bedroom pictured *at right* is a hand-carved pine bed, brought up to date with a flower-strewn contemporary linen pattern. At least a century separates the bed and its clothes, but the spirit is uncluttered country all the way. A few select country pieces, showcased against neutral walls and well-waxed wood floors, create a look that's almost Shaker in its simplicity.

Two features that country rooms have in common are their honesty of material and simplicity of line. Old country pieces started life as utilitarian items; newer versions maintain that down-to-earth look.

The carving on the bed shown here is about as elaborate as a country piece is likely to get. The pine table and chair beside the bed and the large but unadorned mirror behind them also make a typically restrained statement. A cream-colored rag rug warms the wood floor both literally and figuratively; in keeping with the rest of the room, it's attractive, but neither flashy nor luxurious.

Remember that country is a broad term that applies to more than one type of room. Although a clean, uncluttered look is typically country, another person's version of the same style might include many more collectibles—old bottles, woodenware, assorted candlesticks, crocks, toys, dolls—and an assortment of colors, such as soft, deep reds and blues.

When grouped together, even a few collectibles can make a clear decorating statement and do much to set the mood of a room. The duck decoy resting on an old cheesebox in the foreground gives some hint of the decorative accents that are right at home in a country-style room.

MODERN

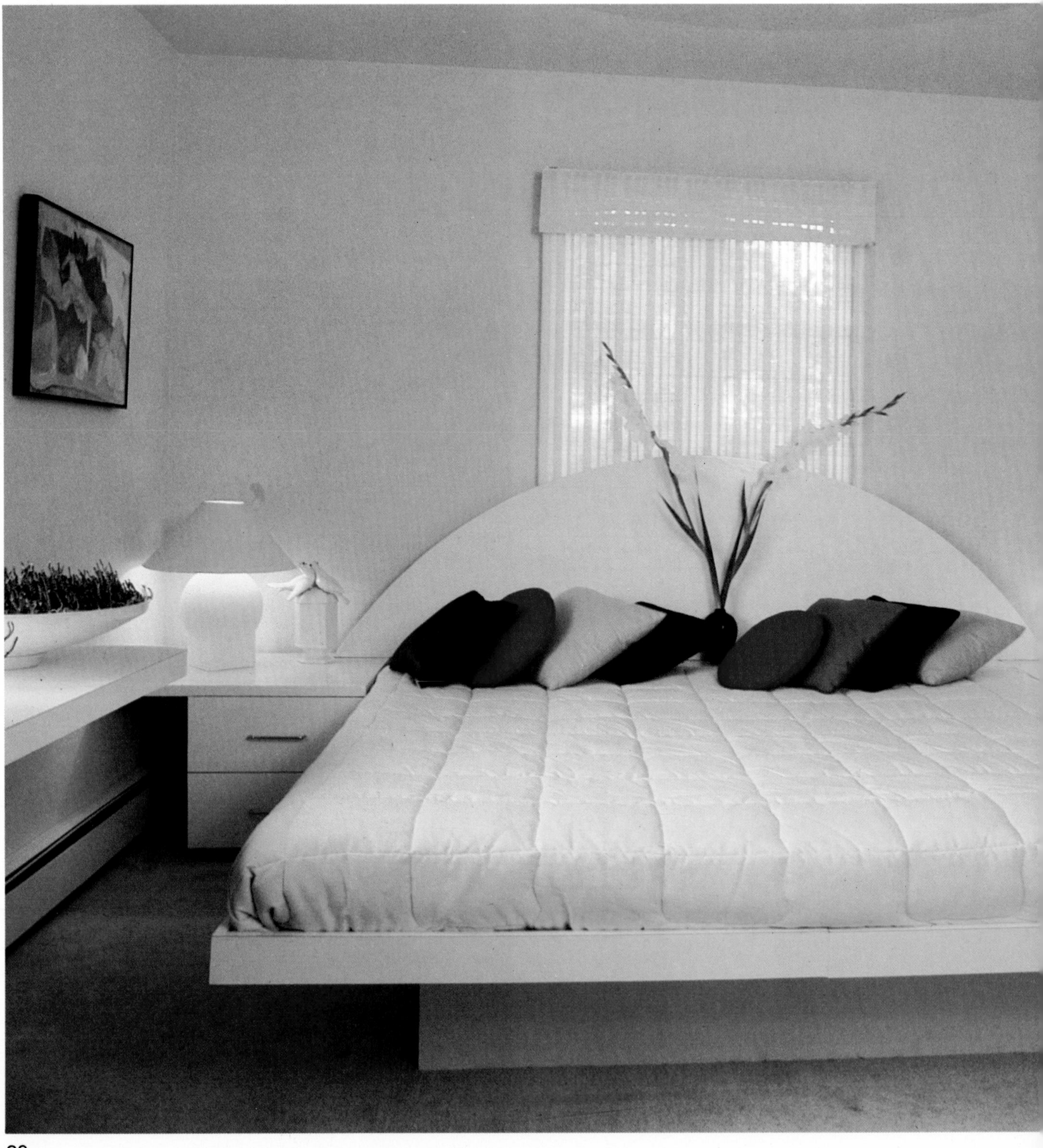

Purity of form, clarity of function, and a lack of superfluous accessories are among the trademarks of modern rooms. Depending on the furnishings used, modern settings can appear to be either casual or formal. But whatever their degree of formality, modern settings all have one characteristic in common: a restful tranquility derived from simplicity itself.

Modern design traces its roots to the Bauhaus School of the 1920s—a German academy of art, architecture, and design founded on the credo, "Form follows function." And when that credo is adhered to, the result is likely to be a serene, clutter-free room, a haven carefully designed around a few well-chosen pieces of furniture.

The pure geometry of modern furnishings ranges from the hard-edged look of steel-framed Bauhaus chairs to softer curvilinear designs. In the bedroom pictured *at left*, for example, the broad sweep of the half-moon headboard lends an unexpectedly romantic 1930s air to the cantilevered platform bed.

As with all good design, materials in modern settings are usually honest and straightforward; they don't pretend to be anything but what they are. Here, for example, the major furniture pieces are covered in pure-white plastic laminate.

Although chalky white-painted walls once were *de rigueur* in modern settings, color is making a welcome comeback. This room's surprising pink walls warm up what might otherwise have been a bland rectangular space. Color also provides a dramatic backdrop for the curved headboard.

In keeping with the streamlined mood, modern window coverings are generally spare and trim, without extraneous decoration. Simple, uncontrived treatments—a roll-up shade, an accordion-fold fabric Roman shade, plain wooden shutters, or clean-cut vertical or mini-slat blinds, for instance—provide adequate privacy and light control without overpowering a stripped-down setting.

COLORING
A ROOM

There's more to coloring a room than making sure that colors don't clash with each other. Color, carefully selected and imaginatively used, can visually reshape an awkward room, brighten a stingily windowed one, or cozy up a formal and austere room. Best of all, color can do all this at the stroke of a paintbrush or the toss of a pillow or two. The more you know about what color can do in a bedroom and throughout your house, the better you'll be able to use it. Here and on the next seven pages, we'll give you a short course about color, how it affects space, and how you can use it as one of the most effective decorating tools.

How you use color is much more than a matter of what your favorite colors are and how certain colors make you feel. Colors, and the intensity or subtlety with which they're used, have a lot to do with your perception of a room's size and proportions.

Light colors recede; dark ones advance. White or off-white opens up a small space by visually pushing back the walls; darker colors help make an oversize room seem cozier.

Using more than one color on the walls or ceiling can minimize awkward proportions, too. For instance, you can "square up" a tunnel-shaped room by painting the long walls white and one or both of the end walls a bright color. And you can visually lower a too-high ceiling by painting it a darker color.

When it comes to choosing colors for bedrooms, how you use the room has a lot to do with your decisions. If the room doubles as an office or hobby spot, warm, bright colors will add cheeriness and stimulation. If, on the other hand, your bedroom is mainly a place for quiet relaxation and reflection, cooler, calming hues can establish a serene mood.

A bedroom that gets a lot of daytime use probably will look best in light colors. If your bedroom doubles as a breakfast or brunch spot, yellow can add a welcome sunny touch. If you often use your bedroom for evening reading or television watching, darker hues can create a sheltered feeling.

Keep in mind, too, that colors can make a room seem cooler or warmer. Try warming up a wintertime retreat or a room that receives only cool, northern light with yellow, orange, or red. Or, add refreshing blue or green to an overly sunny, south-facing space.

Color basics—more than basic colors

Check the color wheel shown *opposite* and you'll see that colors fall into three general categories—*primary, secondary,* and *tertiary*—with the secondaries and tertiaries falling in between the primaries. In a sense, primaries, secondaries, and tertiaries are spokes on the color wheel. On our wheel, *tints* of these colors fall near the hub and *shades* are out toward the rim.

Achieving a pleasing color scheme demands that you use *complementary* colors judiciously, as explained at the hub of our color wheel. For harmony, choose tints and shades of the same color, or colors that are near each other on the wheel.

The particular color or colors you select can mightily influence how a room looks. To show you the magic that color can work in a bedroom, we've colored the same room with three very different schemes. Six pages of variations of that same bedroom begin when you turn the page.

(continued)

COLOR BASICS

When you think of colors, perhaps the *primary colors* come to mind first. These—red, blue, and yellow—are the strongest.

The *secondary colors*—green, orange, and purple—are created by mixing equal parts of two primaries.

Tertiary colors—such as yellow-orange and blue-green—are created by blending equal parts of a primary color and the secondary color containing it on the color wheel.

When you mix secondary and tertiary colors that are close neighbors on the color wheel, you get a restful scheme.

Tints, created by adding white to any color, and *shades,* colors to which black has been added, can be major ingredients of any color scheme. For example, a room decorated in tints and shades of blue offers a great deal of visual variety, but because the "colors" are all variations on the same color, the effect often is peaceful and relaxed.

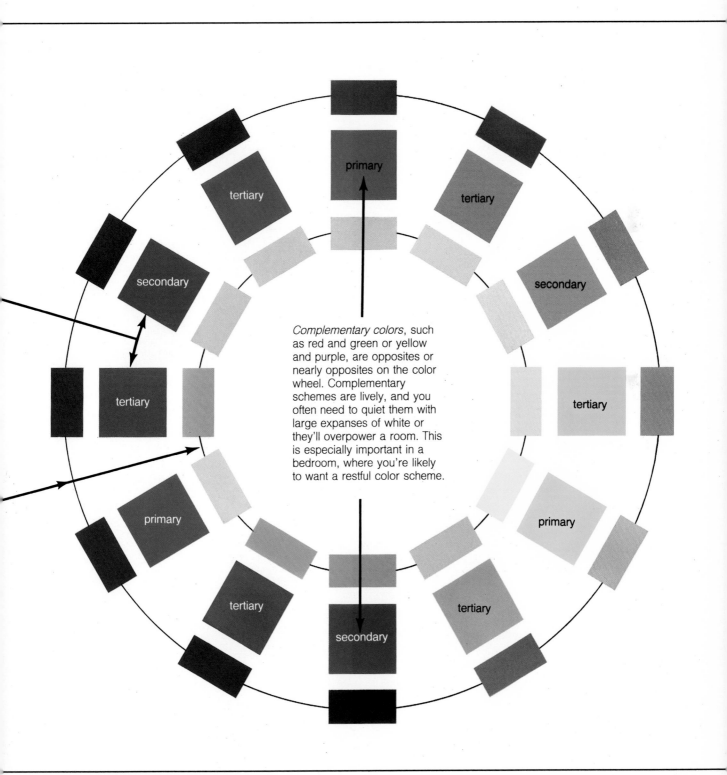

Complementary colors, such as red and green or yellow and purple, are opposites or nearly opposites on the color wheel. Complementary schemes are lively, and you often need to quiet them with large expanses of white or they'll overpower a room. This is especially important in a bedroom, where you're likely to want a restful color scheme.

primary

tertiary

tertiary

secondary

secondary

tertiary

tertiary

primary

tertiary

tertiary

secondary

COLORING A ROOM: NEUTRALS
(continued)

If you've always thought of neutrals as bland (and maybe a little bit boring), think again. These easy-to-live-with color schemes can be a visual and tactile delight.

Take a look at the bedroom pictured *at far right*. Light, airy, restful? Yes. Bland? Definitely not. The room owes its airy sophistication to a confident use of white; mellow woods and textures contribute country-style warmth.

Here the walls and ceiling were painted white. Not only does this give the small space an expansive look, but white's reflective quality also makes the most of incoming light from the room's only window.

The difference between a neutral scheme that's dull and one that has real punch is texture. Here, the knotty grain of the plank flooring and antique washstand play off the matte-white walls. Even the dado, although painted white to blend with the walls, adds a measure of rough-sawn texture to the scheme. To complete the tactile variation, there's the slick sheen of the painted metal bed, the brass lamp, the mini-slat blinds, and the glass over the framed doilies.

The swatches shown *at near right* illustrate cool and warm variations on the neutral theme. *At upper right,* nubby blue-gray carpet, shiny glazed cotton fabric, and white-and-gray grid wallpaper provide a cool neutral look. For a warmer effect, you might look to the rich brown carpet, subtly patterned wallpaper, shiny painted shutters, and nubby woven fabrics pictured *at lower right*.

(continued)

COLORING A ROOM: WARM TONES
(continued)

There are no hard-and-fast rules about the colors that are "right" for any given space. Even in a small room, the effect you seek may be coziness, not expansiveness. In this version of the same bedroom shown on the preceding pages, yellow, contrasted with crisp white, warms things up.

Here the golden walls and carpeting advance into the room, encircling the bed with snug comfort. Generous use of white on the lacy bedclothes, bedstead, and rocker keeps the yellow from overwhelming the room.

A much darker shade of yellow on the dado and crown molding adds architectural interest and dimension. Note how the dark-painted dado seems to come forward into the room, while the paler walls above it recede.

Warm variations

One way to vary any color scheme is with pattern. Just take the colors from a single pattern, and use them to color your room. The swatches *at upper near right* are one example. The patterned fabric, a camel, gray, and white leafy design, might be used for the bed's comforter. For flooring, a gray-tone carpet echoes the gray in the fabric. Then, for contrast, paint the walls and shutters a light-camel tone and use a subtly striped gray fabric for the bedskirt and pillows.

Or, as shown by the swatches *at lower near right,* you could choose a warm-tone rusty-brown carpet to anchor the scheme. Over the windows use mini-slat blinds in a light-camel color that match the walls. Finally, dress the bed in complementary plaid fabrics.

(continued)

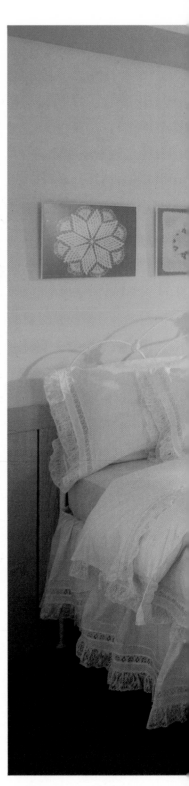

COLORING A ROOM: DRAMATIC DARKS

(continued)

Our third version of the same bedroom, pictured *at far right,* shows how you can effectively use one strong, dark color to create a sheltering ambience. Against the richly colored background, the white furnishings and window trim stand out clearly, and the patterns of the framed doilies are even more vivid.

Dark colors camouflage imperfections and variations in texture. The dado, which had been emphasized by the paint treatment in the yellow room, now almost disappears under its coat of dark green paint.

In a room like this you may want to paint the ceiling white to reflect maximum light. A contrasting paint treatment also offers a way to lower a too-tall ceiling: Stop your dark wall color a few inches below the ceiling and paint the resulting border to match the ceiling. Or paint the ceiling and border a darker hue than the walls.

Try dark patterns

When you're working with dark colors, patterns are a good source of subtle variations within a color scheme. The swatches shown *at near right* also show that you can use more than one pattern in a room, as long as they share compatible colors.

The swatches *at upper near right* show a woven window shade that adds tactile appeal, and reverse versions of a grid pattern for the walls and bed. Light beige carpeting, reflecting light, would make the room seem larger.

At lower near right, a darker salmon-hued carpet swatch goes nicely with luxurious floral drapery fabric. To dress the bed, consider a subtly striped fabric in a dark-beige tone that picks up the beige in the drapery fabric.

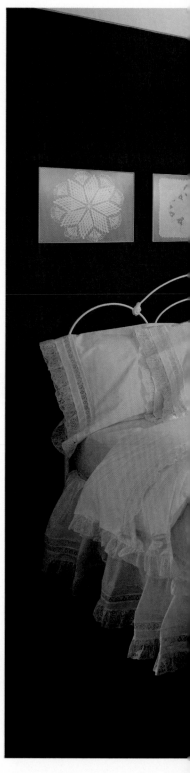

36

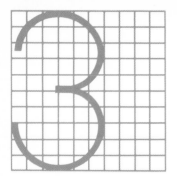

PLANNING A MASTER BEDROOM

Although most master bedrooms do contain a large bed, there's more to planning this important room than simply moving in a mattress. The term master bedroom conjures up images of space—enough room for an armchair or a private bath, if you don't already have one. In this chapter we'll tell you how to tailor a bedroom to your specifications, starting with space utilization and traffic patterns. After the basics, this chapter moves on to the finer points that set the master bedroom apart from standard sleeping quarters.

SIZING UP YOUR SITUATION

Unlike the owners of the master bedroom shown *at right,* you may not have a fireplace and molded mantel in your bedroom. But the restful color scheme and gracious details that do so much to make the room inviting are the results of imagination and careful planning, not architectural good fortune.

Before you get serious about planning your own master bedroom project, you'll need to make a detailed assessment of the area you have to work with. A good floor plan will help you pinpoint where the best opportunities are for the transformations you have in mind.

Start with a pencil, graph paper, and measuring tape. Note locations of window and door openings as well as room and furniture dimensions. Scrutinize possible traffic patterns, but don't be restricted by them. Because a master bedroom gets so much less traffic than a living or dining room, for example, you can be more flexible in your furniture arrangements. A coffee table or love seat placed at an unexpected angle in a master bedroom probably won't get in the way, as it might elsewhere.

Next make a list of features you'd like to have. If you want a spa or private dressing room, now's the time to try to plan one. Consider pulling down nonbearing walls, for example, or converting closets into work space. Once you've determined your wants and needs, try to find a way to accommodate them.

PLANNING A MASTER BEDROOM

EXTRAS

Learning to think like a designer will open your imagination to the multitude of improvements that can be made to the bedrooms at your house. Once you are familiar with the basics discussed on the preceding pages, turn your attention to extras—such as a vanity, a walk-in closet, or a dressing area. On these two pages we show three different ways to alter the same master bedroom. Each calls for only minor remodeling, and all work within existing space.

Before planning major revisions to a bedroom, ask yourself if simply rearranging the furniture could make a dramatic difference. Minor changes in the room's layout can make major improvements and could save you the expense of more substantive alterations.

If more than just a new furniture arrangement seems needed, reshuffling a few walls or closets could provide the extras you'd like to have. For inspiration and some down-to-earth ideas as well, study the examples shown here. Starting with the "before" plan, *above right,* we show how one room configuration can be altered to accommodate several extra features.

In the original floor plan, the master bath adjoining the bedroom (partially covered by the tissue paper) includes a lavatory, toilet, and tub. A long closet with bifold doors is to the left of the bedroom door, with the bed along the wall to the right.

The first revision, shown in the plan, *lower right,* eliminates the lavatory in the original bathroom, making it possible to shorten the bathroom several feet. This in turn frees space for a new vanity/lavatory in the bedroom itself. A dressing table beneath the window and a dresser in the corner give the room a custom-designed dressing area. A folding screen between the bedroom and the vanity provides inex-

pensive and attractive instant privacy.

The second variation, *above left,* incorporates into the master bedroom both a dressing space and a seating area. Again, the floor plan is altered very little. The lavatory moves out of the existing bathroom into a dressing "hallway" created by enclosing the space around it and the dresser. Moving the bed nearer to the dressing area makes room for a comfortable seating group to the right of the bedroom door.

Improvements in our third version, *below left,* include a walk-in closet and a home office, complete with desk and bookshelves. This time the bath keeps its original shape, but a short wall (an extension of one wall of the new closet) creates a niche for the dresser. Part of the original closet remains, and overall hanging space is more than doubled, thanks to the new walk-in. Although there's less floor space in the bedroom, there still is

plenty of room for the bed and night table on the wall opposite the closet.

How can this work for you?

For minimal to moderate expenditures of money and effort, each of these plans offers an efficient use of once-wasted space. Seeing the several options on paper may help open your eyes to even more possibilities.

Other simple alterations can maximize space, too. For example, rehang doors to swing in the opposite direction from the way they do now. Removing an old, unused fireplace can create more usable wall space. Relocate radiators or heating ducts if they're inconveniently placed. Build a loft for your bed to free floor space below. Or place the mattress on a storage base, eliminating the need for a dresser. Any of these changes would be considerably less expensive than adding on to your house. Try to think of other ways to get the extras you want in your bedroom without paying extraordinary amounts to do so.

PLANNING CLOTHES STORAGE

Even the most confirmed clutterer may be tempted to reform if supplied with a storage system where everything really does have a place. Without adequate storage, your bedroom will inevitably be strewn with shoes, shirts, and assorted accessories. A sensible storage system not only will make your room tidier, it will extend the life of clothing because clothes look better and last longer if they're given "breathing room" in the closet.

The spacious dressing room pictured *above* takes out all the potential for clutter in the master bedroom by providing a separate storage area. In this case, the owners worked with existing space adjacent to their attic sleeping quarters to create a superbly organized open storage system.

How large *your* storage area needs to be depends on what you want to store. Take stock of your belongings, and decide whether seasonal items should be stored elsewhere when they're not in use.

Allocate specific amounts of space to specific items, and allow a few extra inches for getting the contents in and out. Group your items by size. Consider adding drawers or shelves beneath shorter items hanging on a closet pole or add a second-tier closet pole to double your hanging space.

The kinds of belongings you'll be storing will determine the type as well as the amount of storage you'll require. For example, tightly closed storage is important to protect woolen items from moths in warm weather. If you have a lot of

suits or dresses, hanging room rather than shelf space will be at a premium.

Types of storage

Each bedroom in your house, including the master bedroom, probably already is equipped with a basic shallow closet—typically, 24 inches deep and 5 to 8 feet wide. Closets like this offer lots of room for improvement. If the closet has sliding doors that always seem to be in the way, think of replacing them with bifold doors.

Surprisingly, walk-in closets offer less storage per square

foot than do their shallower cousins. Why? Because walk-in closets need a 2-foot-wide corridor for access. Converting a walk-in closet 4 to 5 feet deep with access on both sides to a pair of shallower back-to-back closets will increase storage. If this isn't feasible, install closet poles along the longer wall or walls. The two illustrations *at right* show how making these changes in a walk-in closet maximizes storage possibilities.

Shelves along the back or on one wall of a closet can hold folded clothes, eliminating or reducing the need for space-robbing dressers in the bedroom itself. Space shelves about 7 inches apart.

Don't neglect the shelf possibilities above closet poles. Boxes holding seasonal or rarely worn items will be out of the way yet accessible on upper closet shelves. If there's room, install a second shelf about 12 inches above the first shelf.

An array of ready-made storage units can help you customize existing closet space even further. Choose from wire baskets, clear plastic shelves and trays, or even wooden shelf systems in a variety of dimensions. Some glide on runners, others are stationary or supported in their own freestanding roll-around frames.

If existing closet space isn't sufficient, look to the room itself. Open shelving is relatively inexpensive and easy to install—but prone to collect dust. Cabinets provide more protection and are available in a range of sizes up to massive wall-filling wardrobes.

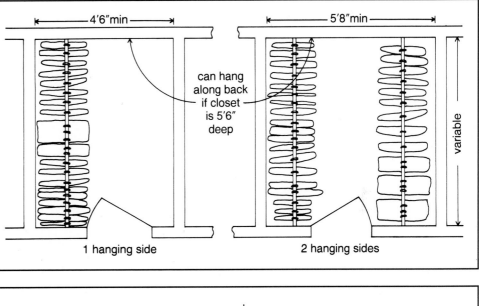

4'6"min

5'8"min

can hang along back if closet is 5'6" deep

variable

1 hanging side

2 hanging sides

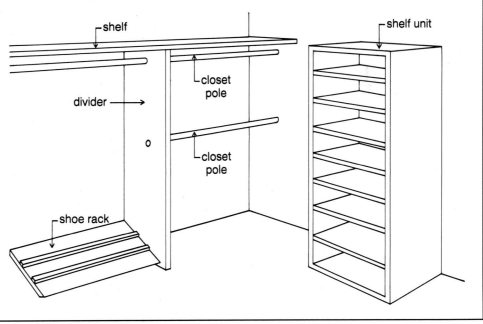

shelf

shelf unit

divider

closet pole

closet pole

shoe rack

REMODELING CASE STUDIES

On this and the following three pages, we'll examine some master bedroom remodeling plans. Each of these case studies illustrates how to find additional living space within a home's existing structure. Remodeling can involve anything from adding a closet to an existing master bedroom to creating a new master suite from two smaller rooms. Sometimes just moving an interior wall a few feet redirects traffic so dramatically that the room easily takes on a new role. This kind of structural change is considerably cheaper to make than to add on new square footage.

BEFORE

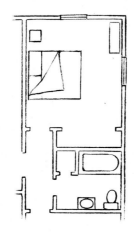

AFTER

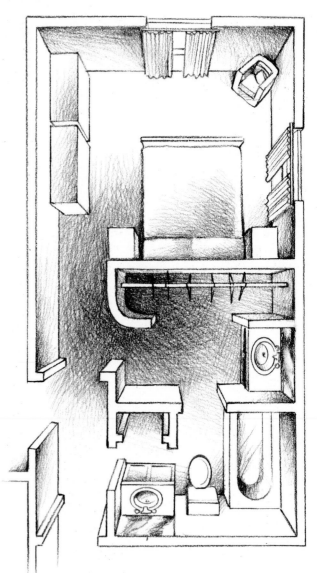

The small plan *above* shows a fairly standard master bedroom layout—two access doors, two windows, and a shallow closet. In the adjoining bathroom, a tub and shower were on one wall and a toilet and pedestal lavatory on the opposite. This bath allowed only one-at-a-time use—no private dressing area, no his-and-her vanities.

The large plan *at right* shows an imaginative and relatively inexpensive solution. Expanding and reorienting the closet created a new walk-in dressing room. The new layout also features a compartmentalized bath that's more comfortably shared by two. Moving the tub to the outside wall and adjusting the position of the toilet created a passageway into the bath from the new dressing room. A lavatory replaced the pedestal sink, and a second, larger vanity was installed in the dressing area.

The bedroom lost a few square feet, but the added wall space allows for a new, more efficient furniture arrangement. There now is room for a second dresser and another bedside table.

A private master bath is one of life's most satisfying home luxuries—but the facility off the master bedroom in the "before" plan shown *at right* made an unfortunate compromise on the way to providing this nicety. It included only a shower stall and lavatory; the toilet and tub were in the main bath down the hall.

The bedroom's awkward traffic flow also reflected poor planning. The room lacked a dressing area, and the long, narrow closet opened right inside the bedroom entry. The floor plan accommodated only one chair comfortably, allowing no space for a reading corner or table.

As in the remodeling on the opposite page, this redesign required relatively minor wall changes. The closet was moved several feet and the access now faces the bath rather than the sleeping area. The result: a new dressing room.

Eliminating the clothes-closet bottleneck not only makes the bedroom seem bigger, it also helps it function better. The wall space gained by altering the closet provides a new location for the dresser. Moving the dresser frees a corner opposite the bed for a pair of chairs and a small table.

BEFORE

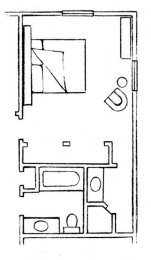

Adding a toilet to the master bath was the major improvement in this remodeling project. Removing the shower stall and transferring the lavatory made enough room for both the toilet and the new tub/shower combination. A pocket door installed between the dressing room and bathing area provides privacy without taking up the space that a conventional swinging door would.

The convenience and comfort the full private bath provides more than offsets the investment required for plumbing. The expense of additional plumbing can be minimized by locating new fixtures as close as possible to existing plumbing. Plan the bath so it adjoins another bathroom, or position it directly over a downstairs bath or kitchen to minimize pipe runs.

When you're planning new plumbing features, you may want to go beyond the basics. For example, a whirlpool soaking tub could be installed in a bathroom this size, creating a spalike setting.

AFTER

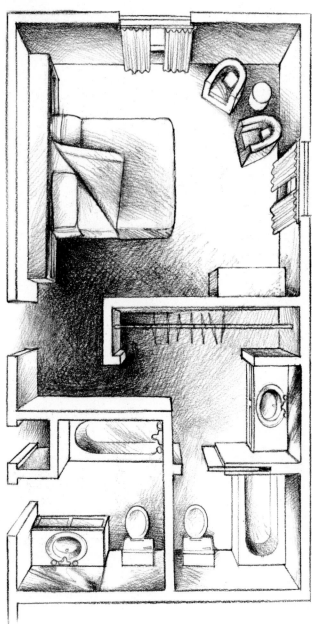

REMODELING CASE STUDIES
(continued)

AFTER

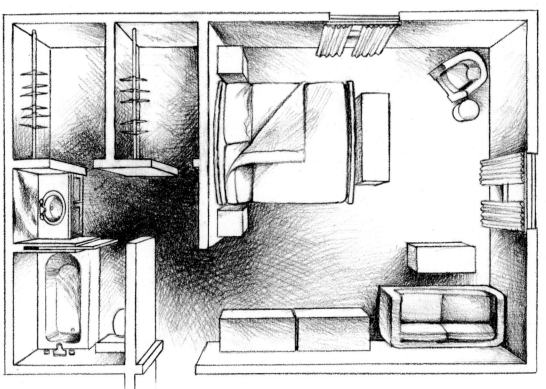

Y ou *can* improve on a good thing. The master suite in the "before" plan shown *at right* has all the basics in place—a full bath with modern fixtures, a walk-in closet, and a sitting area.

Yet, even with these pluses, the room's layout was less than ideal. With no passageway between the bath and closet areas, the bedroom became the dressing area. The walk-in closet, although spacious, did not offer enough space for his-and-her storage or for stowing out-of-season items.

The new arrangement, shown *above,* trims a few square feet off the bedroom area. The loss of floor space is hardly noticeable, and what's

been subtracted from the bedroom adds dramatically to the comfort and convenience of the entire suite.

As the new plan shows, a compartmentalized arrangement, with the toilet/tub area separated by a pocket door from the lavatory alcove, made a big difference in the layout. Juggling the position of the bathroom fixtures allowed direct access from the bath to the closet area. The resulting passageway and sheltered floor space between the closet area and bath becomes a natural dressing area and keeps all the clothes clutter out of the bedroom.

By pushing the closet wall a few feet into the bedroom, one oversize closet was converted into two generously proportioned side-by-side closets. A dresser and shelves at the back of one of the closets hold folded items and shoes.

Repositioning the closet door created a long unbroken wall in the bedroom. Moving the bed to the new wall and the dressers to a side-by-side arrangement next to the hall door made room for several additional pieces of furniture. A lift-top chest that doubles as informal seating now holds linens at the foot of the bed, and a chair and table fit in the corner, with room to spare for the sofa and coffee table opposite.

BEFORE

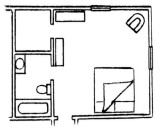

AFTER

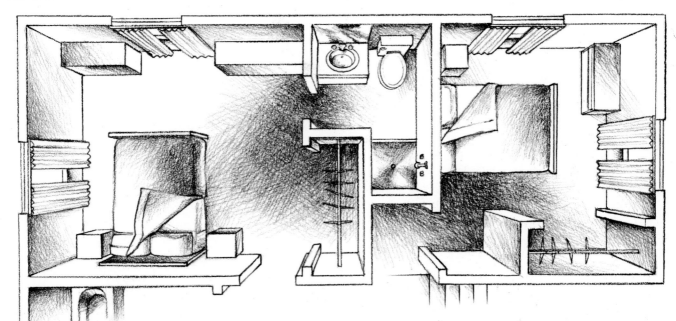

As the "before" plan *at right* shows, the original bedrooms in this second-story "dormitory" area were almost equal in size and quite serviceable. Like many second-story bedroom areas in older homes, however, this sleeping zone had no bath at all. The nearest bathroom was downstairs and around a corner.

When the house changed hands, the new owners wanted to create an upstairs master bedroom with private bath and retain a guest room with access to an extra bath. Although each of the original bedrooms had windows on adjoining walls for good light and ventilation, neither had star quality or presented obvious qualifications for use as the master bedroom. Therefore, creating baths and a new master bedroom upstairs

demanded a revision of the entire floor plan.

Beginning with plumbing, the most expensive item, the homeowners reworked the layout. The upstairs hall closet, with ample space for a tub, toilet, and lavatory, was located directly above the downstairs bath. This made it the logical spot for a new bathroom. The new tub is partly visible at the bottom left of the new layout.

To achieve master bedroom proportions, the walls of the room on the left side of the plans were moved several feet, taking some space away from the bedroom on the right. The guest room is still comfortably proportioned, with its own

closet and enough space for a double bed and other essential furnishings.

The closet that once served the bedroom at right now serves the master bedroom. An extra few feet also were commandeered beyond the old closet to make room for a shower stall, toilet, and lavatory; together they form a compact but convenient three-quarter bath. By locating this bath directly over the kitchen, plumbing and new pipe runs were kept to a minimum.

The master bedroom, though not grandly proportioned, is spacious enough to accommodate a double bed, two night tables, two large dressers, and a closet. A pleasant alternative arrangement might replace one dresser with a small sitting area in the corner between the two windows.

BEFORE

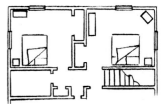

ADDING ON

Yes, we have said that the ideal way to plan a master bedroom is to work within existing space. It's cheaper, easier, and often neater. But what if you simply can't rearrange furnishings, use built-ins, or design clever storage to capture the square feet you need? What if the judicious removal of a wall or two isn't enough? Then adding on, for all its expense, hard work, and major planning, probably is the answer.

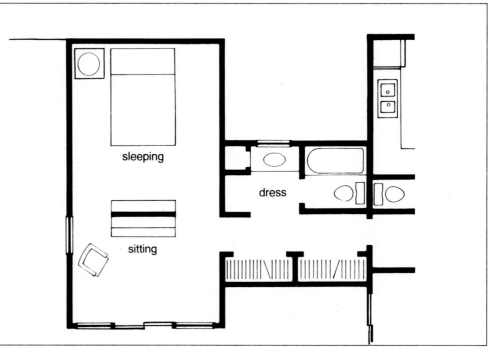

sleeping

dress

sitting

A
lthough adding on costs more than remodeling within an existing space, it's often less expensive to add on than to buy or build a new home. And often even a modest but carefully planned addition can turn your present home into the one you've always wanted to live in.

Before you decide to add on, there are some things to stop and think about. Consider comparable houses in your neighborhood, increased property taxes, and resale potential. An addition will increase the value of your house, and that may be a good thing. But you may not want to improve your house so that it's substantially more expensive than other homes in your neighborhood. You'll also have to consider building codes and lot-line restrictions, and the demands of dealing with banks and a remodeling contractor.

Once you decide to take the plunge, you have a variety of options. Should you add out or add up? Should you match the existing house style and material, or try for contrast? Whatever you do, you won't want to spend thousands of dollars for an addition that makes your home more spacious but less attractive.

When you're planning a master bedroom addition, privacy and quiet are more likely to be important than when you're adding on a family room or new kitchen. The example pictured *opposite* and in the floor plan *above* shows how a master suite can be tucked behind the main structure, creating a welcome refuge from family activity.

As the plan illustrates, an existing corridor leads into the addition. Beyond the corridor, a full bath/dressing room and 11 feet of storage space flank a second passageway. The new master bath shares a

"wet wall" with a bath in the existing house, minimizing plumbing costs.

The new entry creates a practical buffer between the master suite and the rest of the house. Beyond the entry, the new wing widens to accommodate a sleeping area as well as a sitting/reading/TV area. A freestanding divider separates the room into two zones and provides additional storage space.

The exterior treatment, pictured *opposite*, is carefully designed to harmonize with the existing house. New and old roof pitches and roofing materials are identical. Big, to-the-eaves windows brighten the sitting area and sliding glass doors open to a deck that wraps around two sides of the addition.

PLANNING A NURSERY

A helpless infant soon becomes a wonder of locomotion in search of adventure, so plan your nursery for safety, convenience, and flexibility. Keep walls, floors, and furnishings as childproof as possible to protect the child from its surroundings and vice versa.

Your first nursery acquisition probably will be a crib. If your baby's "nursery" will be beside your own bed, a rocking cradle like the one shown *at far right* will serve during the first few months. Or choose an item that can grow with the child, such as the versatile crib/chest shown *at right;* it converts to a bed with separate drawers.

All new cribs sold in the United States meet standards set by the Consumer Product Safety Commission. According to the standards, the maximum spacing between slats should be 2⅜ inches; otherwise, a baby could get its head caught between the bars. In addition, all cribs must have a two-stage catch to lower a side. The mattress and the inside dimensions of the crib must be the same; 27½ inches by 51⅞ inches has become the standard size. If you're considering a secondhand bed, check for slat spacing, stability, smooth surfaces, lead-free paint, and a snug-fitting mattress.

If you don't plan to use furnishings for later children, choose simple pieces that will work as well in a six-year-old's room as they do in an infant's. Then dress up the room with appropriate accessories, such as the "Gladys Goose" lamps shown here. Cords should be out of reach and exposed electrical receptacles covered with safety shields.

Look for multifunctional pieces that can grow with your child. For example, the dresser *at right* features a changing tabletop that can later hold an older child's grooming aids.

Like the toy chest in the photo, storage items should be scaled to a small fry's height. Make sure chest lids have safety hinges so small children can't be injured.

EXTRAS
FOR KIDS

Children's sleeping places lead active daytime lives, too—as fantasy lands and play areas for small fry, then later as studies and teen entertainment areas. Imaginative room designs with creative ''extras'' help rooms keep pace with growing children, and make them more fun to live in.

Younger children need lots of play space, with room to spread out toys and games. For older children, whose interests focus more on hobbies and collections, storage space becomes crucial. And for teen-agers, work centers and lounging areas take precedence.

Each of the rooms shown here demonstrates how an ordinary bedroom can offer extraordinary possibilities. The skylit hideaway pictured *opposite* is well equipped to provide both privacy and play space, thanks to a divider wall outfitted with pocket doors. When the doors are open, the 14x14-foot room becomes a generously proportioned play room for two boys; when the doors are closed, there's plenty of individual space for sleeping and studying. The sleek birch built-ins for each child include a ladder-access bed, a desk tucked under a window, and tall storage shelves.

Two for one

A flexible, portable wall on wheels shown *at upper right* is an ideal part-time divider for an undivided or shared room. Built with eight hollow core doors, plywood shelves, hinges, and casters, this unit provides walls, storage and display space, and a desk. The hinged doors can be rearranged for various room configurations, and the shelves and desk are adjustable. The entire unit folds together and rolls out of the way to maximize open floor space.

In the room shown *at lower right*, two youngsters have their fair share of stowaway space built into the walls adjoining their study space. Wall-hung bookcases flank the double-desk width of laminate counter. A trundle bed saves precious floor space.

59

PLANNING CLOTHES STORAGE

Closets usually are the focus of attention for clothing storage in children's rooms and guest bedrooms. Unfortunately, there's no foolproof formula for The Well-Organized Closet; what works for a teen won't do for a toddler or an overnight visitor. Take the time to plan clothing storage with a customized approach. The payoff is tidier rooms, more relaxed guests, and youngsters who can find their own clothes.

If your children can't reach the clothes in their closets because the poles are set at grown-up heights, you're doomed to putting their clothes away for them until they're tall enough to do better.

Get down to your kids' level to evaluate their clothing storage needs. Keep storage low-slung to encourage independence and responsibility at a young age.

The nifty doorless closet shown *opposite* makes the point; this young girl has three closet poles within arm's reach. Two shelves for storing extra toys, sweaters, hats, and more are within her reach. A layer of clear plastic boxes on shelves organizes shirts and underclothes in an easy-to-find manner.

Closet doors may be welcome in an older child's room and can be added later, but leaving the doors off very young children's closets gives them the easiest access to their belongings and encourages tidiness.

The chart *at right* illustrates child-scale heights; use these as a guide when you're planning clothing storage for your youngsters.

The best storage systems for children are modular units with movable shelving that adjusts to meet children's changing needs and sizes. When selecting dressers and other storage pieces, look for ones you can add on to later. For easy care, pick furniture with painted or laminated surfaces, or all-plastic construction.

Make room for guests

Unless your guest room is occupied regularly and often, a guest closet should be multifunctional. But because of space shortages elsewhere in the house, many people treat the guest room closet as the final resting place for all kinds of seldom-used items. When a visitor has no place to hang clothes because broken fishing rods and stacks of old magazines take up the entire closet, it's time to sort things out.

Because most of us are short on storage space, we need an extra closet for spill-over storage. To make room for both guest and household storage, divide closet space into separate zones for guest needs and for storing your own belongings, such as seasonal clothing.

You can use double-tiered closet poles to good advantage here, efficiently storing short items such as shirts and jackets. Consider installing some built-in shelves or ready-made wire baskets or plastic shelving in part of the closet to organize craft or hobby gear, sewing supplies, or home office needs. Or hang pegs and dowels to support sports equipment such as skis and tennis rackets.

Review your annual guest list. Does it mainly include weekenders who travel light, or do guests stay for several weeks? Depending on how long guests stay and how much clothing they bring with them, they may be able to manage with just half of a clothes pole and one wide shelf. For long-term guests, you'll need to make other adjustments to keep your guest room closet well-organized, spacious, and gracious.

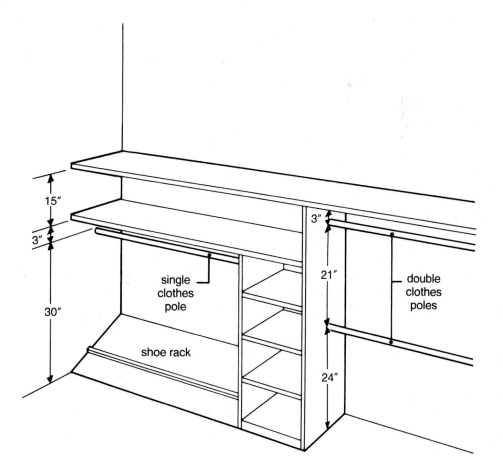

15"

3"

30"

single clothes pole

shoe rack

3"

21"

double clothes poles

24"

REMODELING CASE STUDIES

The best-laid plans for both children's rooms and guest rooms take a multifunctional approach. Children's spaces need to accommodate playing and studying as well as sleeping; guest quarters often serve primarily as home offices, craft centers, or dens. Furthermore, they often have to handle all these activities in a limited amount of space. Here and on the following pages, we take a close look at four different remodelings of children's and guest bedrooms, showing how each faced the space-squeeze challenge. If the problem looks familiar, study the plans to see if you can adapt our solutions to your situation. In each of these cases, the remodeling solution works within the existing space, keeping costs and remodeling chaos to a minimum.

The first question to ask yourself is: Can I accomplish my goals within the existing space? To help find the answer, draw a detailed floor plan of the room on ¼-inch graph paper and note all pertinent dimensions. Then turn to pages 156 and 157 and trace the templates of furnishings you'd like to use. As alternate possibilities occur to you, select additional templates. You may want to exchange a bunk bed for a double bed, for example, or twins for a double.

The "before" plan on this page shows a standard layout for a 10x10-foot guest or child's bedroom. Twin beds flank a small night table, with a dresser in the corner next to the closet.

The problem: how to pack versatility into the same area. As long as the space-gobbling bed arrangement remained, there was little hope of getting more function from this room. But switching to a Murphy bed opened the floor plan to lots of space-expanding possibilities.

Placing the new Murphy bed on the wall to the right of the entry door leaves the center of the room open for activities, and makes the room appear larger than it is. Murphy beds are available from a number of manufacturers; most come with a spring-loaded prebuilt frame and standard hardware. (If you'd like to build your own Murphy bed, see pages 136 and 137.)

We added a sofa for extra seating on the opposite wall. Or, to accommodate one more guest, set a twin mattress with a fitted cover on a platform and let it double as bed and sofa.

A new built-in storage system was designed to wrap around the sofa, vastly improving the room's storage capaci-

AFTER

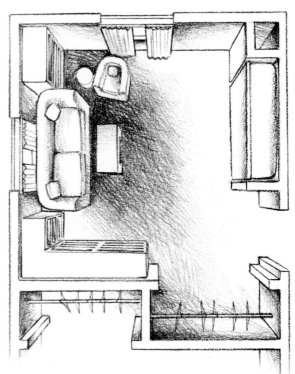

ty. The units could be floor-to-ceiling height for maximum storage. If the room is for a young child, plan low-to-the-ground storage such as rollout bins in the bottom half of the unit, and reserve the top section for display or for storing seasonal and infrequently used items. A pull-down surface in one or both of the units creates a perfect spot for children's homework or adults' desk work.

The room still has lots of usable space. Here we filled it with an extra chair, a coffee table, and a side table and turned it into a cozy teen-age retreat or a friendly guest room. If the room is intended for small children, keep the floor space clear for active play or large toys such as a rocking horse or dollhouse.

BEFORE

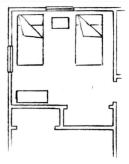

Whether used as a child's room or as a spare bedroom, the room shown in the "before" plan *at lower right* doesn't live up to its potential. Three pieces of furniture—a twin-size bed, night table, and dresser—nearly fill the room. A shallow closet consumes the remaining wall area. Crowded sleeping space and boxlike proportions give the room little intrinsic appeal. Clearly, an innovative solution is needed.

One way to improve a room such as this is with built-ins. Like the room on page 62, this space could be put to work with a variety of built-in units or ready-made modular pieces that offer floor-to-ceiling storage. When floor space is limited, built-ins that go up rather than out use available wall space efficiently.

The solution illustrated here combines a budget-watcher's frugality with a designer's eye for space planning. A skilled do-it-yourselfer easily could execute the removal of walls, framing, and finishing work. Even if you need a carpenter, no expensive electrical or plumbing changes are likely to be involved.

The first step was to eliminate the closet on the right wall and build two closets with total storage space equal to the previous one. This created a cozy niche at the head of the bed. If the room were to be used as a guest room or home office, one of the closets could be fitted with shelves to store supplies and papers rather than clothing.

The old closet wall became the background for a special-task corner equipped with a desk for study, sewing, or hobbies. The desk features built-in shelves and drawers. In a child's room, the desk surface could be designed to adjust to higher levels to keep pace with a growing child.

The new design makes a flexible room plan that, with minor decorating and storage adjustments, will be as comfortable for a teen-ager as for a toddler. As a spare room, it provides a comfortable retreat for sewing or studying. And the ample closet and wall storage create space for essential materials in the same room where they're needed.

Stretching strategies

An eye toward space-conscious decorating can help you make the most of any modest-size bedroom. Use light, space-expanding colors rather than dark ones that visually draw the walls in. Avoid sharp color contrasts between the floor, walls, and ceiling. Separate blocks of color break up a room and make it look smaller.

Choose streamlined, lightly scaled furnishings instead of heavy, ornate pieces that can gobble up visual space. Opt for versatile pieces wherever possible, such as a desk that doubles as a dressing table, or a storage platform that puts space under the bed to good use.

Keep accessories and clutter to a minimum. Use a tailored bedspread rather than a frilly one, and treat your windows so they blend into the background.

AFTER

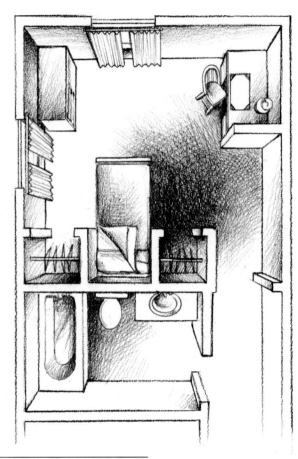

BEFORE

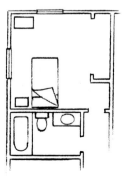

REMODELING CASE STUDIES
(continued)

In houses where separate bedrooms for each child seem like luxuries, it's not always easy (or even possible) to achieve the ideal bedroom arrangement for everyone, but there are ways to make the best possible use of space.

The remodeling shown on this page proves that bigger isn't always better, or even necessary. By dividing one large room, you may be able to conquer the not-enough-space problem without the expense of building an addition.

The stairs in the "before" plan indicate that this is a second-floor or attic space. (You could use a basement this way if exit and window requirements can be met, but as a rule spaces below-grade are not acceptable for bedrooms in single-family dwellings.) The original space is generous enough, but lacks privacy; the solution begins by carving the large rectangular room into new shapes.

A partial partition divides the center of the room lengthwise. Beds placed side by side in this central section are nestled into niches created by right-angle extensions of the new wall.

Doors at the entrance to each bedroom ensure privacy. The shared area adjoining the old closet is an ideal play space, since it's located in neutral territory.

Each new room has its own clothes closet, and the old closet has become an oversize toy chest. As the children get older, it could be converted to store stereo equipment, books, or sports gear.

BEFORE

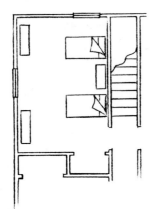

Putting up a partition of this kind doesn't involve structural work. Depending on your skills and the time available to you, framing and finishing the new partition and closets and adding the built-ins could be a totally do-it-yourself project. Or you may prefer to have the framing work done and do the finishing yourself.

Finishing touches to a project of this type go beyond painting the walls. Think of adding blackboards, bulletin boards, or wallpaper to one wall. Brighten the room with bedding, window treatments, easy-care floor coverings, and good lighting.

The "after" plan offers several other possibilities for space-efficient sleeping. The beds could be bunk beds, providing room for overnight guests. If ceilings are high enough—a real possibility in the center portion of an attic—consider elevating the beds to serve as sleeping lofts, with built-in desks and bookcases below. Ladders and safety railings are musts.

AFTER

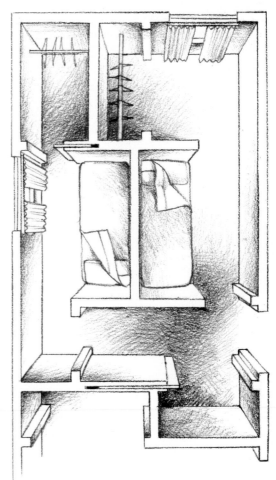

The children's rooms shown in the "before" plan *at right* have a lot going for them. Both are roomy and private, and located out of the mainstream of household activities. However, the homeowners wanted to alleviate traffic jams and short tempers outside the family bathroom door during the morning rush hour. They did so by carving out a bath for the children and taking over the original bathroom for themselves.

Finding room for a full bath for the children without sacrificing the spacious layout posed a challenge. As the "after" plan shows, some bedroom space was given up, but that didn't mean sacrificing any quality in the remaining space.

The new bedrooms, although smaller than the originals, have more closet space. Switching furniture around created interesting layouts and compensated for the slight loss in square footage.

The twin beds, formerly at right angles to inner walls, were shifted to the outside corners of each room and angled to keep valuable floor space open for play areas. Each bedroom has space for a chair and table, large dresser or desk, and nightstand or bookshelf. The small closet units that originally divided the two bedrooms were moved and expanded.

The bath, centrally located between the two bedrooms, is accessible from both. A door separates the lavatory from the toilet/tub area. The extra-large vanity provides enough counter and storage space for two children. Additional storage space (not shown) is available in the hall, convenient to both rooms.

BEFORE

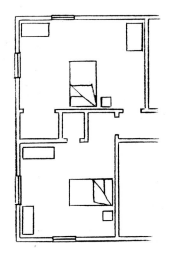

What makes a children's bath?

When you're planning a bathroom just for children, make sure it's easy to take care of, with waterproof surfaces throughout. Mopping up will be easier, and more likely to be done by children themselves, if you forgo the pile carpet.

When very young children or toddlers are sharing a bath, safety is a vital consideration. All the safety pointers that apply to any bathroom take on even more importance when children are involved. Keep medicines and cleaning supplies somewhere else. Choose a nonslip floor covering and put a nonslip rubber mat inside the tub. Provide a step stool that can be moved from the toilet to the sink.

Adding a bath can be expensive under any circumstances, but adding one within existing space is less costly than a room addition would be. If you can tie into plumbing directly above or below the new bathroom, you'll save a lot of aggravation and money.

AFTER

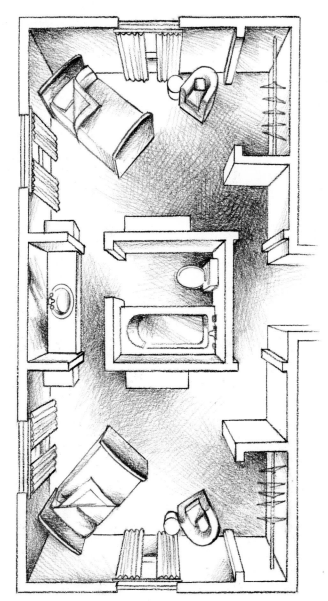

ADDING ON

As your family grows and you need more room, you may finally reach a point where using space efficiently and decorating to enlarge a room visually still don't provide enough space. If you don't want to move, you may decide the time has come to add on to your house. An architect or qualified remodeling contractor can help you design new space that functions with flair.

An addition can be anything from a small bay window or dormer to a whole room or wing. Whatever its size, a well-executed addition will alleviate storage and traffic problems at your house, make living there more pleasant and convenient, and provide the new space you need.

Depending on your house's architecture and local zoning laws, additions can go up or extend from the sides, front, or back.

Building in the backyard

The addition shown on these pages is an ambitious one: a two-bedroom children's wing that opens off the back of a 1950s-style house. Its location out of the mainstream of household traffic means that the new wing doesn't disrupt existing living patterns, nor do adult activities disturb the children after bedtime. Direct entry from the deck and the garage to a conveniently placed mud room helps minimize traffic through the house.

The corridor that leads from the main part of the house to the new wing occupies space taken from a half bath. Realigning fixtures and displacing a linen closet made room for the hall without sacrificing the half bath.

There's a new three-quarter bath in the addition; an auxiliary heating unit and storage for play and sports equipment are in a utility room between the bathrooms.

Although the bedrooms are compact, careful planning and

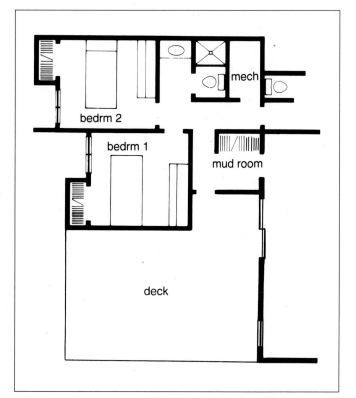

styling make them seem more spacious than they really are. Built-in beds and study/storage units make excellent use of available space and give the rooms a sleek and tidy appearance.

Asymmetrically arranging the rooms in relation to each other and to the rest of the house created a structure that frankly admits it's an add-on. Vertical natural wood siding minimizes exterior maintenance.

Other directions for adding on

Adding on to the sides or front of a house can be more trouble than you might think. Setback restrictions, mandated by zoning, specify the minimum distances between a structure and its lot lines. Many homes already are perilously close to these minimums.

In a single-story house, or a two-story with a commodious attic, adding *up* might be the answer. In a ranch, for example, you might choose to raise all or part of the roof to create children's sleeping space.

Or consider adding a new master suite and converting your existing master bedroom to sleeping space for one or more children. This might make special sense if you currently don't have a true master suite with its own bath. To learn about adding a master suite, see pages 52 and 53.

A BEDROOM FOR A WHEELCHAIR USER

To design a comfortable and convenient bedroom for a wheelchair user, you must select and adapt furnishings and fittings that will both accommodate the bulk of the chair and be within reach of the seated person. Here we offer general guidelines that you can customize to suit the individual needs of the person or persons who will be using the bedroom.

Half a million disabled men, women, and children in this country are confined to wheelchairs. In addition, thousands of elderly people depend on wheelchairs at least part of the time. If you or a member of your family uses a wheelchair, you know that a conventionally designed and furnished home can be difficult and frustrating to maneuver in.

For maximum convenience, a wheelchair user's bedroom should make the most of limited reach and mobility. This means carefully selecting all the details—floor coverings, bedding, lighting, furnishings, and storage.

Floor coverings must be level and easy to negotiate. Avoid deep pile, plush, or shag carpets. Hard surfaces, or commercial grade carpets with a tightly looped pile, provide smooth finishes, are durable enough to withstand friction, and allow a wheelchair to roll easily. Avoid loose area rugs and eliminate raised door thresholds wherever possible.

Good access means open traffic lanes. Barrier-free passage for a wheelchair user requires a minimum of 5 feet square for turning around. Doors must be at least 34, and preferably 36, inches wide. Bathroom doors should swing outward.

Bed and beyond

A platform bed is a good choice because its recessed base accommodates the wheelchair's footrest. Most disabled people find a double bed more comfortable than a twin size, and if more than one person will be using the bed, you'll probably want at least a queen-size bed.

To facilitate getting in and out of bed and bedmaking, a wheelchair user needs a minimum of 44 inches of clearance at the end of the bed and at least one side. Choose a tailored, fitted bedspread with no draped fabric to catch in the wheelchair mechanism.

The bed shown *opposite* has a headboard high enough to provide adequate back support yet low enough to be used as a grab bar when needed. The bedside table is about 6 inches higher than the bed—a height that's easy for a reclining person to reach. A sturdy table large enough to store a phone, books, tissues, and drinking water is ideal.

Walls covered with a commercial-weight vinyl wall covering can withstand bumps from a wheelchair. Windows and their coverings should be simple to open. Instead of curtains or draperies, you may choose mini-slat blinds which can be ordered with an extra-long tilt wand for easy reach.

Storage units should be low and sturdy so they won't tip over if a person leans or pulls on them for support. Open shelves offer easy access. Install low closet bars so a seated person can reach them without straining.

Select chairs and sofas with arms for support when pulling up to transfer to a wheelchair or to stand up. Upholstery that "breathes" makes long hours of sitting more comfortable. A leather armchair with a slick surface, such as the one pictured *at upper left,* makes it easier to slide in and out.

Good lighting is essential for safety. Switches should be installed low, and placed so lights can be turned on before entering the room, and turned off from the bed. Lamps with switches on the cord, rather than on the lamps themselves, are easier to operate. A telephone and intercom add additional convenience.

NUMBERS TO KNOW

Use the following dimensions as guidelines in planning or converting a bedroom for a wheelchair user.

The average wheelchair is 27 to 29 inches wide. For easy passage, doorways should be 36 inches wide and hallways 48 inches wide. Narrower passages make it difficult to maneuver the wheelchair. Pocket doors, which disappear into the jamb rather than fold against the wall, can sometimes alleviate the problem of narrow clearance in a hallway.

Doorknobs or lever handles should be 36 to 39 inches from the floor; window controls should be 56 inches or lower.

Counter tops or sinks are best placed 34 inches or less from the floor. A free space underneath the counter or work area should be at least 36 inches wide and 27 inches tall.

Place clothes rods 36 to 48 inches from the floor. The top shelf of a closet should be 54 inches or less, with shelf depths of 16 inches or less.

In the bathroom, the toilet seat should be 19 to 20 inches high; lavatories should be 34 inches or less from the floor and extend 27 inches or more from the wall. Shower stalls must be at least 4 feet square with a front opening at least 36 inches wide.

The most convenient chair seat height is 16 inches. Tables should be 28 inches high and no wider than 42 inches to accommodate the wheelchair user's reach.

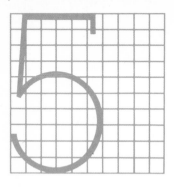

ALTERNATIVE SLEEPING STRATEGIES

As you've learned from the two preceding chapters, the "best" sleeping arrangement for any room depends on who will be using it and how often, and the size and shape of the space itself. From lofty hideaways for children to a grand master suite to a nostalgic room for Grandma, this chapter presents nearly a dozen different sleeping alternatives you can adapt for the bedrooms at your house.

AN 8x9-FOOT BEDROOM

Don't let a bedroom as small as 8x9 feet cramp your imagination. At first glance it may seem that the only way to arrange the furniture is to place a single bed along one wall and squeeze a dresser and perhaps a straight-back chair into the remaining space. But take a second look. You probably can come up with a better arrangement and gain seating and storage in the bargain.

The room shown on these two pages illustrates one dynamic improvement on a traditional arrangement. A platform bed, shown *opposite,* projects diagonally into the room from a corner with adjacent windows. Under each window and snug against the walls, chests of drawers provide storage. Triangular storage cabinets join the chests and the head of the bed. Each cabinet has a convenient niche for nighttime reading material.

Can you imagine a guest bed in a room this size?

Presto! The end of the bed's platform flips up and a guest bed rolls out on casters. Placing beds end-to-end on a diagonal is the only way to fit two beds into such tight quarters.

In another corner, opposite the foot of the bed, *below,* a built-in L-shaped bench provides comfortable seating. The bench tops flip up for access to storage bins.

An open-shelf unit adjacent to the seating-storage unit houses records and books, and there's room for stereo equipment on top.

With most of the furnishings hugging the walls, the open floor space in the center of the room creates an almost spacious look—cozy rather than cluttered, compact and convenient rather than cramped.

Color, too, helps stretch space here. Extensive use of light tones visually pushes back the wine-red walls. Covering the windows with shutters rather than fabric further streamlines the room.

A BED
IN A CLOSET

Closets have been known to hide everything from clothing to the family skeletons, but not many people think of closets as desirable places to lay their heads. If space is limited, however, closets offer interesting alternatives. A readily available bed tucked away into a closet is a great convenience in an efficiency apartment, a child's bedroom, or a living room that doubles as a guest room. These pages show two different space-saving ways to turn closets into sleeping accommodations.

Children are almost invariably attracted to lofts, niches, and cubbyholes—any place they can crawl into and call their own.

The peak-roof sleeping closet pictured *opposite* incorporates the best of several worlds into what was once an 8x8-foot attic storage space. It's private, large enough to allow its 14-year-old occupant to store a few treasured possessions near the bed, and even has a window to provide natural light and ventilation.

The bed snuggles up against one knee wall, allowing safe headroom where it matters. A chest provides both storage and decoration. A basket and low bench along the wall opposite the bed, occupying space that would otherwise go to waste, give the teenager extra niches for books and collectibles.

A bed behind closed doors
The long, narrow living room shown *above* handles overnight guests with ease and discretion. A Murphy bed concealed in a built-in closet is the key.

To make room for the bed, a second wall was built at one end of the room. The new closet is 24 inches deep and runs the length of the wall. A 42-inch-wide center section, which houses the Murphy bed, separates two 33-inch-wide closets that store bed linens and clothing.

The interiors of the closets and bed alcove are finished with 1x8-inch tongue-and-groove siding to match the walls of the living room, as shown *above right*. For stability, the interior surfaces of the closet doors are reinforced with 1x3s nailed in a Z-shaped pattern. This keeps the doors straight and contributes to the country look of the room. When all the doors are closed,

as they are in the photo *above left,* the end wall matches the other walls of the room and there's no trace of the concealed "bedroom."

More about Murphy beds
The Murphy bed, invented by William L. Murphy, is a bed that folds or swings into a closet when not in use. You can still purchase Mr. Murphy's invention at furniture and department stores. The units are available with concealing cabinets, or you can buy just the flip-up bed frame and construct your own enclosure.

If you'd like to add a pulldown bed to your home, turn to pages 136 and 137 for advice. The bed shown *above* attaches to the wall where the headboard would be on a conventional bed. You could install a Murphy bed to attach along the length of the bed, if that arrangement fits better in the room you have in mind.

ALTERNATIVE SLEEPING STRATEGIES

A ONE-ROOM APARTMENT

Sleeping in an efficiency apartment can be anything but efficient without a convenient solution to the sofa/bed dilemma. It's not always easy to make a quick change from sofa to bed and back again. The sofa bed shown here is a double bed that works daytime as a sofa. But you also can meet the challenge of sleeping in your living space with a specially designed sofa that moonlights as a bed. And of course the ideas shown and discussed on these pages can be just as convenient in a study or living room that does double-duty as a guest room.

The trick to sleeping and living in the same room is to keep the bed from looking like a bed when it's not used for sleeping.

The bed turned sofa
The strategy in the apartment shown here is to take the path of least resistance. The bed stays a bed; it just looks like a sofa during the day. A full-length bolster, *opposite,* divides the mattress into two sides of seating. Pillows, featured *at right,* are placed against the bolster to add comfort and visual interest.

Your choice of bed can simplify things considerably. Choosing a platform bed, for example, gives you a head start, since its clean, angular lines look at home in a living room. Use a fitted, quilted mattress cover for the upholstered look of furniture. For more daytime camouflage, heap the bed with cushions, pillows, and bolsters for back rests. That way, it not only looks like a sofa, it functions like one, too.

Another option is to build a bed platform with a raised back along the length of the bed. For comfortable sitting, add thick cushions in front of the backrest to reduce the depth of the bed. Storage units at the short sides of the bed can serve as headboards by night and coffee tables by day.

For tips about sewing covers for pillows and bolsters, see Chapter 7.

The sofa-turned-bed
The alternative to the bed used as a sofa is a piece of furniture that really is a sofa (or chair)

but converts into a bed. Several styles, ranging in size from twin to queen, convert into comfortable sleeping units.

When shopping for a sleep sofa, make mattress quality your first criterion. Don't settle for an uncomfortable bed just because you like the sofa.

Be sure the mattress has the firmness and quality you want. Also consider convenience. Some folding mechanisms are easier to operate than others.

Another option to the traditional pullout convertible sleep sofa is a unit made of upholstered high-density foam. Foam sofas come in two or more pieces that fit together like a puzzle to form a bed and several sofa variations. You also can select modular units of sofas and ottomans that can be pushed together to form a bed.

With all these convertible variations, consider whether you can leave linens on when you convert the bed back to a sofa. Making and unmaking the entire bed can be tedious if you have to do it every day.

LOFTS

If you have a bedroom that's short on floor space and a family member with a head for heights or a sense of adventure, think about creating a sleeping loft. Lofts are increasingly popular as original features in new homes, and it's not hard to add a loft to an existing room. You don't *have* to cut through ceilings or have unusually high ceilings to carve out a loft. These two pages illustrate different loft solutions, each added long after the houses were built, to maximize bedroom space.

Even in a room with a standard 8-foot ceiling, you can build a glorified bunk bed with all the appeal of a full-fledged sleeping loft. The project shown *above* takes a little imagination and carpentry work, but not much space.

The arched balcony facade conceals a carpeted platform supported by a 2x4 frame within the space a standard bunk bed would occupy. The lower portion, designed as a bed, is a plywood platform built on top of 2x12s set on

edge. The framework of this unit was made of 2x12s and 2x4s, and the structure was covered with drywall. A ladder at the left end of the tower leads to the great play space on the upper level. For overnight guests, a comfortable and easy-to-lift foam mattress fits right over the platform.

Still more dramatic possibilities arise where there's more space to reach into, as in a bedroom directly below an attic. In the room shown *opposite,* the original ceiling was opened to the roof line and

skylights were added. Besides making the bedroom larger and lighter, this remodeling created a dramatic play loft on the upper deck. The result: a quiet-time bedroom perfect for sleeping, storage, and studying, and a separate play area on the upper level where toys and games rule.

A bright red metal ladder turns access into fun and a matching railing adds safety. The rope version of a firehouse pole makes speedy descents possible.

BUNKS AND
BUNK BEDS

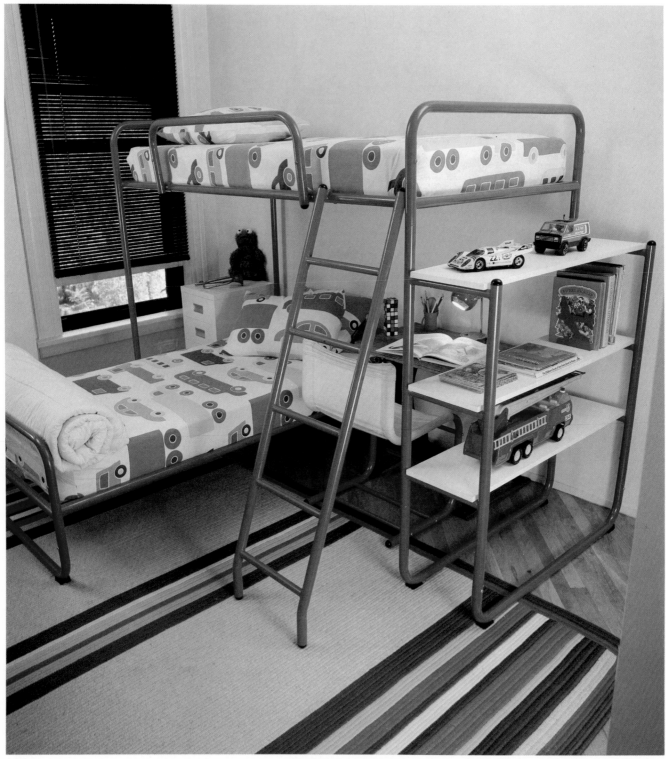

Bunks, which come in standard twin size and also more compact sizes, have long provided efficient, inexpensive sleeping in dormitories and military barracks. Stack one bunk atop another and you have a bunk *bed*—a classic solution to billeting two children in a medium-size room. The floor space you gain with a bunk bed scheme leaves lots of room for toys, books, and play. Here are some suggestions that can help create a bunkhouse at your house.

The colorful bedroom on these two pages belongs to two children. As you can see in the photo *opposite*, the lower bunk bed is perpendicular to the one above. This arrangement leaves enough room for a desk and chair to tuck in next to the bed. Although the beds are close to a window, the open, tubular structure of these beds keeps them from obstructing the light and view. This is a good feature to keep in mind if you have awkwardly placed windows and can't figure out where to put the bed or beds without blocking them.

There's just enough space between the bed and the window for a small file cabinet. It provides extra storage and doubles as a night table.

Storage and safety

Efficient and abundant storage, whether for a toddler's trucks or a teen-ager's stereo system, is a vital element in any child's room. Here, adjustable shelf units, shown *below*, meet the needs of all children's age groups. The lower shelves are deep enough for inexpensive, practical storage bins that keep shoes and clothes orderly and within easy reach of

kids still learning to dress themselves. As with the bunk beds, the practical shelves can be grouped as space and demand dictate.

Safety is an especially important factor where children are concerned. Here, for example, the upper bunk bed has protective railings at both the ends and outer side, and the sturdy metal ladder attaches to the bed frame. The lightweight storage bins on the shelves are easy for children to pull out; because the bins are set low to the floor, they won't injure a child who pulls them out too far.

EXPANDING A MASTER BEDROOM

Do you dream of a home office, hobby corner, exercise center, or TV and reading nook in your master bedroom? Reluctant to add on? Look around. Maybe, as in the dramatic conversion shown here, the space you need is right next door. Or perhaps you can gain valuable space by bumping up or out. Here is a look at ways to expand a master bedroom.

Once you start thinking of a master bedroom as more than a basic bedroom, you may very well want more space or the illusion of more space. A master bedroom, however, doesn't have to be enormous; with the right arrangement, you can create enough space for a sitting/reading corner as well as the basic bedroom furnishings in a 12x15-foot room.

Dividing existing space is one way to maximize usable square footage without actually adding to it. A low divider can subtly but effectively define sleeping and other areas in an average-size room.

Another way to create the illusion of more space is to let more light into the room. A skylight can add a bright new look to any room. Similarly, adding or enlarging windows brightens a room and makes it seem bigger. And if the windows you add are glass doors that open onto a patio or deck, your bedroom can gain a piece of the great outdoors.

The room next door
If you truly need more space, first consider whether you can annex it from an adjacent room.

Examine the floor plans and you can see how the new master bedroom pictured *at right* developed when an 11x12-foot bedroom joined forces with a slightly larger adjacent room. One original bedroom remains a sleeping area; the other, separated by the lower half of the old wall, now serves as a study. Bookshelves and a built-in desk are anchored to the low wall.

In an older home with small, dark rooms and a chopped-up second-floor plan, removing part or all of a wall can make a big difference at relatively little cost. (To learn what's involved in removing a wall, turn to pages 88 and 89.) If rooms already have adequate light and ventilation, you may prefer to leave walls largely intact and connect previously separate rooms with a pair of French doors, pocket doors, or a graceful archway.

Sometimes the space you're looking for is not around the corner but over your head. If there's an attic above your master bedroom, consider removing the ceiling and creating a sleeping loft. The space beneath the loft could become a sitting or storage area.

In an upstairs bedroom, it may make sense to break through the roof with a dormer that provides a welcome pocket of additional space.

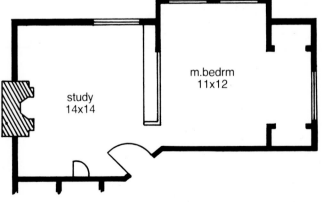

study
14x14

m.bedrm
11x12

CREATING
A BED/BATH
COMBINATION

Need a master bath but don't want to steal space from the bedroom? Or maybe you already have a bedroom with its own bath, but both seem undersized. Combining a master bath and bedroom into one room lets each area borrow visual space from the other, and turns an ordinary master suite into a sumptuous personal retreat.

The elegant and comfortable bed/bath suite shown on these pages started out as two separate spaces. The new layout was created by removing two partitions to integrate the bath with existing bedroom space. With the walls removed, the combined area became a spacious 14½x25-foot suite.

In the photo *above,* the slightly lowered ceiling and marble floor mark off the old, separate bathroom. In the remodeling, three clerestory windows were installed in the bath area to provide light without compromising privacy. Other additions include a pair of shell-shaped pedestal lavatories and a whirlpool tub. The toilet and linen closet tuck into a semiprivate area opposite the new tub; a mirror beside the whirlpool reflects the bedroom and adds visual depth to the area.

Adding a master bath

If you don't already have a private or adjacent bath, creating a master suite will be more complicated and costly. Consider annexing a large closet or part of a hallway and turning it into a bathroom; more ambitious approaches include adding out onto or over a porch or garage, or building a dormer. Opening the ceiling for a sleeping loft might leave room below for a bath.

Whichever bath strategy you adopt, put adequate ventilation high on your list of priorities. This is especially important if you favor an open plan bath/bedroom arrangement such as the one shown here. The sleeping area can become unpleasant and damp if you can't efficiently and quickly remove moisture and odors generated in the bath area. An exhaust

fan is essential, even if the bath area has a window that opens. You also may want a heat lamp over the drying area to ward off after-bath drafts and chills.

If your plans call for a shower, control humidity by including a separate stall isolated from the sleeping area. For privacy, you might want to completely enclose the toilet in its own niche.

At the sleeping end of the bed/bath shown *opposite,* a reproduction antique writing desk and chair, floral bedspread with matching draperies, and ceiling lamp-and-fan combination restate the bath's elegant motif. Your style may be quite different, but whether it's casual, whimsical, sleek, or ruffled, a master bed/bath suite will seem bigger and more luxurious than two separate spaces.

TREAT YOURSELF
TO A SUPER-SUITE

There can be a lot more to a master suite than just a bed and bath. Given space and sufficient funds, you can carry the idea a step further to create a sybaritic super-suite and surround yourself with amenities on a grand scale. Or if this seems beyond reach, borrow a few super-suite ideas to make your room more special.

The 36x36-foot master suite addition shown here has everything. Besides the basics, this suite includes a sheltered whirlpool, screened porch, fireplace, and even a solarium complete with wet bar. The sleeping space is at the center, with the other features arranged around the perimeter for convenience and ease of accessibility.

At the corners of the addition (not shown), two attractive brick enclosures support the roof and contain separate bathrooms, along with necessary mechanical and plumbing equipment. Wiring and ventilation systems span the main room and are masked by wood-sheathed ducts painted a sunny yellow (visible in the photo *at left*).

Suite treats

Behind the fireplace, the solarium, shown *below,* picks up light from a series of skylights installed in the roof. Mirrors on the back wall visually expand this narrow space and multiply the apparent number of plants. At the far end of the room, a wet bar includes an undercounter refrigerator for late-night snacks.

A haven this elaborate is, of course, a major investment. The owners added 1,300 square feet to a home that was originally 1,800 square feet. Their remodeling may be on a larger scale than your budget or lot size permit, but this suite offers numerous affordable ideas that you can pick and choose from to create your very own super-suite.

A MOTHER-IN-LAW SUITE

A mother-in-law suite doesn't have to be for a mother-in-law, of course, but the kind of self-sufficient home-within-a-home that the term suggests is ideal for an older person who has had his or her own home and now needs both companionship and independence. If you're contemplating creating a suite for a grandparent or other adult, these pages will give you some ideas for making a long-term guest feel as comfortable, welcome, and self-sufficient as possible.

The first thing to consider in planning a mother-in-law suite is location. Place the room as far away from the hub of family activities as possible so the older adult won't be disturbed by late-night gatherings or teen-agers' music. You may want to consider soundproofing of some kind. Sound-absorbent ceiling material, thick carpeting, and thick carpet padding help deaden sound.

Try to plan a room with plenty of windows not only for light and air, but also for the view the windows provide. If the room's occupant is housebound or often in bed, windows are especially important. And if this special family member has a green thumb, try to provide good light for plants. A hobby such as indoor gardening becomes even more important to someone sharing another's home.

The ideal mother-in-law suite includes a private bath and dressing area. A compact refrigerator is a nice feature for a snacker, and a telephone in the room, or even a separate telephone line, provides privacy and minimizes conflict.

You might also want to consider supplementing household heat with an electric baseboard unit—elderly people tend to be more sensitive to cool temperatures than younger people. Good artificial lighting and comfortable seating do a lot to make a room more livable, too.

Perhaps the most important feature to include in this room is adequate space for the guest's own things—the belongings that represent the past. Create an environment that reflects individual tastes; the results may be as attractive as the room shown here.

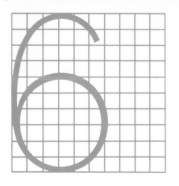

BEDROOM BUILDING BASICS

Previous chapters have shown how small improvements can make a big difference in a bedroom's livability. Removing a wall, building a closet, installing a vanity lavatory, and the five other projects depicted in this chapter tell how to go about doing the work. All are feasible jobs for a moderately skilled do-it-yourselfer. And even if you decide to hire a professional for a particular task, you'll benefit from knowing how work should be done.

REMOVING WALLS

Before you start any project that involves removing or repositioning walls, you must determine which walls are load-bearing and which are not. *Load-bearing walls* are integral elements of a house's structure, and removing or weakening even one can have disastrous results. *Nonbearing walls* simply divide spaces and play no structural role.

To find out if a wall is load-bearing, look in the attic or basement to see which way the joists run in relation to the wall in question. If the joists and wall are parallel, the wall probably is supporting nothing but its own weight; if the joists and wall are perpendicular to each other, the wall could be carrying a load and should be left alone until you've consulted with a professional.

The steps involved in removing a wall are illustrated *opposite*. Removing a nonbearing wall isn't a complex job. You do have to check for electrical circuits, ductwork, and plumbing in the wall, though, before you start demolition. If there's any extensive rerouting involved, consider hiring an expert to do these jobs and handling just the carpentry work yourself.

Once the old wall or walls are out of the way and the new one(s) in place, you'll need to make cosmetic repairs. Floors must be patched, and walls and ceilings touched up—first with plaster or drywall and then with paper or paint.

For a short introduction to what a little wall juggling can accomplish, see the two illustrations *at right*. They're before and after plans of a master bedroom remodeling in which nonbearing walls were shifted to reorganize bed, bath, and storage space.

BEFORE

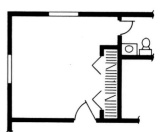

The "before" floor plan *above* shows a typical master bedroom, with one large closet around the corner from the master bath. The room's entry is somewhat abrupt, with the door opening directly into the room. A short closet partition wall blocks both vision and access to the space immediately to the right of the door.

AFTER

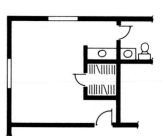

The "after" plan *above* shows a vanity/dressing area, a clearly defined entry, and a walk-in closet. To achieve these changes, the homeowners extended the original closet wall partition farther into the room. The entry door was shifted to the right by several feet, and a new vanity with ample counter space was installed outside the bathroom.

1 Once you've done the preliminary planning and checking, it's time to start work. Wear protective eye and head gear, and spread drop cloths everywhere. Gypsum and plaster dust are difficult to clean up.

Your first step is to remove all door casings, baseboards, and other trim. Work carefully to save as much as possible for reuse. Remove any exposed nails to avoid injury.

2 Pound, pull, or pry away plaster and lath or wallboard—you won't be able to recycle these materials anyway. You'll discover that this part of the job goes quickly, but carting away the debris takes longer. With plaster,

use a shovel to load boxes or barrels. Don't overload containers; plaster is heavy and a full container may be more than you can handle.

3 Before you begin demolition, make sure you turn off any utilities running through the wall you're taking down. Once the studs are exposed, remove any wiring, saving boxes and fittings but not the wire itself. To reroute

electrical, plumbing, or heating runs, you may need to hire a professional.

4 If you carefully take out the framing lumber, you should be able to reuse much of it. To remove the studs, you'll need a hammer and wrecking bar. (A saw will work, but not as quickly.) It's easiest to remove the

studs first, and top and soleplates last. Because these are adjacent to flooring, ceiling, and walls, be especially careful when you pry them off. This will reduce the amount of surface repair you'll have to do later.

BUILDING A CLOSET

Closets seem like fixed, permanent parts of a house, and in a sense they are. But because few play load-bearing roles, closets are easily enlarged, added, or re-located—routine jobs for a professional carpenter, and not difficult ones to master for a weekend do-it-yourselfer.

To construct a closet you'll need 2x4 or 2x3 lumber, drywall or paneling, nails, joint tape and compound for finishing the drywall, and a prehung door unit.

Begin by planning your new closet or closets on paper. (Chapters 3 and 4 explain how to do this.) Then, with a square and chalk line, mark on the floor and ceiling where the new walls will go. This full-size ''plan'' lets you check one more time what the changes you have in mind will do to bedroom space, and also serves as a guide for positioning the new walls' top and bottom plates.

The illustrations on these two pages show our closet, indicated in the diagram on page 88, taking shape. Though you might choose paneling as a covering material, we've elected to present the basics of drywalling.

Drywall has several virtues. It's economical, easy to cut, noncombustible, and noise-retarding. Nailed, glued, or screwed to studs, drywall becomes an integral part of the wall (or ceiling), and provides a smooth surface for paint, paper, and other wall coverings.

Keep in mind that cutting drywall creates a lot of dust, smoothing joints requires that you work with a compound the consistency of gooey mud, and sanding is necessary after the compound has dried. To minimize mess, use drop cloths on all exposed surfaces.

1 First, secure top plates to the ceiling. Where new walls cross ceiling joists, nail into the joists. In other places, use toggle bolts.

2 Double-check the bottom plate's location by dropping a plumb bob from the top plate. Nail plates to the flooring.

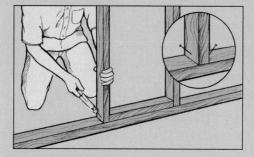

3 Now cut studs to fit between the plates and position them 14½ inches apart. Nail studs to the plates by nailing at an angle.

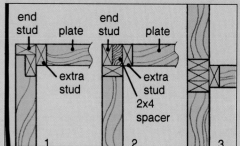

end stud   plate   end stud   plate

extra stud   extra stud 2x4 spacer

1   2   3

4 At corners and intersections of walls you'll need extra studs. Situations 1 and 2 offer other good ways to get around a corner.

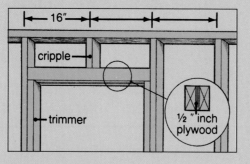

16"

cripple

trimmer

½" inch plywood

5 Top a door by laying 2x4s on edge, with a ½-inch thickness of plywood spacers between them. Secure this *header* with *trimmers* below and *cripples* above.

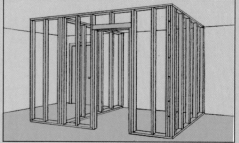

6 Once framing is completed, your new closet will look something like this. As you work, make sure everything is plumb, level, and square.

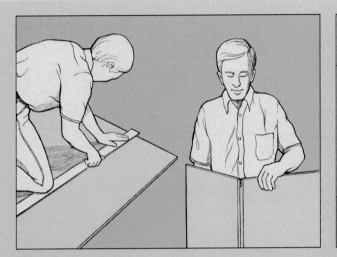

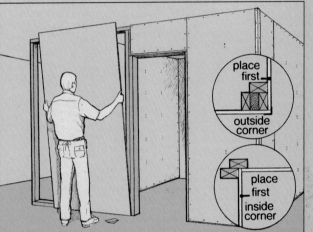

7 Now you're ready to begin drywalling. For straight-line cuts in drywall panels, score through one paper face with a utility knife. Use a metal straightedge to keep the cuts even. Once you've scored the drywall, snap it firmly. The core will break evenly, leaving only a hinge of paper to slice through. Make any curved and complex cuts with a keyhole saw.

8 To put up drywall, place panels against the studs and, every 7 inches, drive a ring-shank nail ½ inch from the edge. After the nailhead is flush with the surface, whack it one more time to form a "dimple" around the nail. Don't hit too hard, though; you don't want to break through the drywall's fragile paper surface. Strengthen outside corners by tacking on lightweight metal *corner bead*.

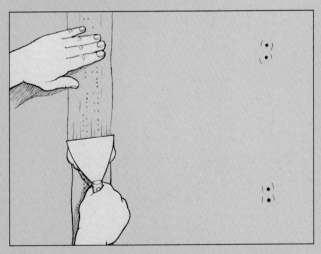

9 Use a 4-inch knife and drywall joint compound to fill the tapered joints between panels. Before the compound sets, apply joint tape, using the knife to embed it into the compound. Fill nail dimples and apply a 4-inch-wide swath of compound along each side of corner beads. After the compound has dried, apply two more coats, lightly sanding between them. The second coat should be 6 inches wide, the third 12.

10 For the door, choose a sliding, bifold, or prehung unit. With a prehung swinging door you set the assembly into the opening— door, frame, and all—then level and plumb the unit by sliding shims between the door's frame and rough framing around the opening. Just a few nails through the frame secure everything. Bifold and sliding door sets are not prehung but come in kit form.

INSTALLING A VANITY LAVATORY

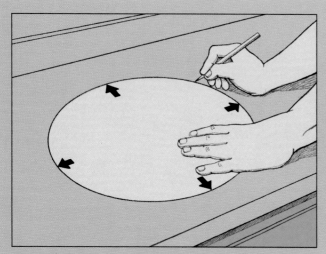

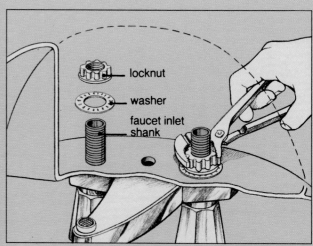

1 Lavatories use one of two mounting systems, rim-type and self-rimming. Self-rimming fixtures, usually made of heavy cast iron, come with templates. Position the template according to the manufacturer's instructions and trace around it. Rim-type basins use the rim as a template; trace around the outside edge of its leg as shown and cut out the traced opening with a saber saw.

2 Next, attach a faucet set to the basin. Fit a rubber gasket over the faucet's inlet shanks, slip the shanks through holes in the lavatory, then fit a washer and locknut onto each shank. Draw up the locknuts hand-tight, then go just a quarter turn further with a wrench; overtighten and you risk cracking the soft brass locknuts. You also can attach a faucet set after the sink is installed, but the job is trickier because you have to work from underneath.

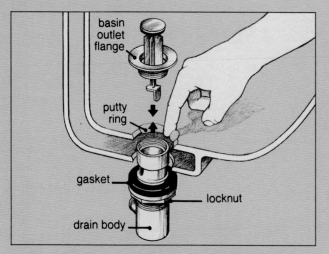

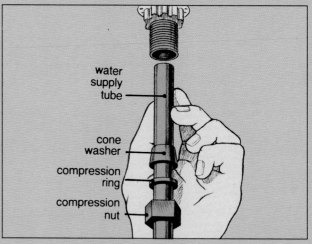

4 Now turn your attention to the lavatory's drain outlet. You need to thread together an assembly that consists of the components shown here. First apply a ring of plumber's putty around the basin outlet, then insert the *flange* into the outlet, and hand-tighten the other parts from the underside. Again, tighten only a quarter turn more with a wrench.

5 To bring water to the faucets, you'll need fixture shutoffs, which attach to the stubbed-in supply lines, and flexible tubing to run from the shutoffs to the faucet inlet shanks. Hook up the tubing with compression fittings consisting of the elements shown here. Maneuver the tubes into the inlet shanks, force the washer, ring, and nut up into each shank, and hand-tighten the nut. Tighten only a quarter turn more with a wrench.

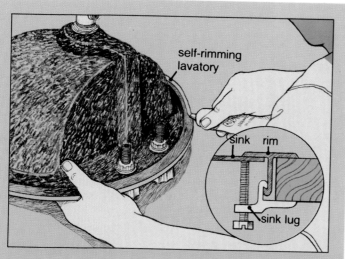

self-rimming
lavatory

sink   rim

sink lug

3 The procedures for setting a rim-type sink vary somewhat, but with most you attach the rim to the sink, drop the assembly through the counter cutout, and secure the unit from underneath with screw-on lugs. With a

self-rimming sink, like the one shown here, you run a bead of silicone adhesive around the underside of the fixture's flange, turn the basin right side up, and drop it into the opening. The basin's weight holds it in place.

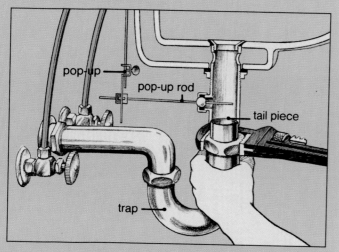

pop-up

pop-up rod

tail piece

trap

6 Finally, thread a *tailpiece* into the *drain body*, connect the tailpiece to a *trap*, and install the *pop-up* assembly that raises and lowers the lavatory's *stopper*. The tailpiece and trap join with a slip fitting; slide a large nut and

rubber washer onto the tailpiece, slip the tailpiece into the trap, and gently tighten the nut. The pop-up assembly goes together as shown. If the stopper leaks, loosen the thumbscrew and adjust the *pop-up rod*.

Installing a vanity unit and hooking up a new lavatory are easy tasks that you can probably accomplish in a single day. However, getting water to and from the lavatory could be an entirely different matter.

The key to a simple hookup is to locate the new unit as close as possible to an existing sink. Examine our installation, shown in the plan on page 88, and you'll see that though there's a wall between the new and old lavatories, they're separated by only a couple of feet. Plumbing codes allow you to hook one lavatory into another's drain line if they're no more than 24 to 30 inches apart (depending on local code). This means that a second unit situated either side-by-side with an existing fixture or back-to-back with a common wall between will require considerably less plumbing work than a new lavatory that's farther away. No sink nearby? You also might be able to tap into a drainage stack serving fixtures on floors above or below. Whatever hookup you decide on, be advised that you'll probably need to apply for a building permit for a new sink installation. The permit application most likely will require a drawing of the arrangement you have in mind. After the permit has been approved and the work completed, a plumbing inspector will check to be sure everything has been done according to code.

If you have doubts about the location you're thinking about, consult a plumber; you also may want to hire him to "stub in" supply and drain lines for your new lavatory. Then you can make the connections shown *opposite* and *at left* without special plumbing skills.

Once plumbing lines have been brought to the location, you need to select or build a vanity cabinet and counter, and purchase a basin and faucet set. Choose the fixture first and then the faucet, which should have inlet shanks spaced to fit holes in the basin. The usual spacings are 4 and 8 inches, though some faucet sets can be adjusted for wider spreads between shanks. Better-quality faucets feature "washerless" design for reduced maintenance.

Vanity cabinets
Prebuilt cabinets are widely available at kitchen and home center stores. Some come with integral tops; for others, you buy the counter top separately.

If you build your own vanity cabinet, make it about 31 inches high, with a back or side that's at least partially cut out so you can make the plumbing hookups.

Set in the cabinet first, use shims to make it level and plumb, then screw the cabinet to studs in the walls behind and/or flanking the unit. Next, attach the counter top of your choice to the cabinet. Don't worry yet about making a cutout for the lavatory. Except with integral basin/counters, you do this *after* the counter is in place, as shown *opposite*.

Why bury yourself under layers of sheets, blankets, and bedspreads when just one lightweight comforter will keep you sleeping comfortably year round? A comforter like the *duvet* (pronounced "doo-VAY") pictured *at left* is so easy to stitch, you can make several to suit the seasons.

Like other comforters, duvets have a light, puffy filling sewn between two layers of fabric, making them comfortable in the summer as well as winter. But the duvet is characterized by the decorative fabric "sack" that encloses the inner comforter.

The duvet cover slips off like a pillowcase, so when it becomes soiled, pull the cover off and put it in the washer.

Before you stitch
To make your duvet, you'll need quilt batting and four flat sheets. Two of the sheets will be used for the decorative outer covering, so they should be of high quality and in a pattern and colors that coordinate with your bedroom. The other two sheets, which will be used for the hidden inner comforter, can be "seconds."

To determine the size of batting and sheets to buy, figure the dimensions of your finished duvet. It should be at least 18 inches wider than your bed and long enough for proper overhang at the foot.

Three of the sheets should be slightly larger than the finished measurements. One decorator sheet should be at least 5 inches longer than the other, so you can tuck in one end of the duvet cover to hold the inner comforter in place. As for battings, they're made for all bed sizes. Choose a batting that's slightly larger than your duvet dimensions.

Creating deep-down comfort
The first step in making the inner comforter is to trim the bargain sheets so they are 1 inch longer and 1 inch wider than the finished measurements of the duvet. This will provide ½-inch seam allowances. Lay the two sheets on top of each other, right sides facing. Then lay the batting on top and pin it in place.

Stitch through the three layers around three sides, leaving one short side open for turning. Turn the comforter right side out so that the layer of batting is sandwiched between the two sheets. Fold in ½ inch on the layers at the open end and topstitch them together.

To keep the batting from shifting, pin and stitch through all three layers in horizontal and vertical rows spaced about 5 inches apart.

Dressing your duvet
The finished duvet cover is made about 1 inch shorter and narrower than the comforter, which will make the comforter fluffier when it's inserted.

Cut one decorator sheet to the same size as the *finished* comforter. This will be the cover's bottom layer. For the top layer, cut the other sheet the same width as the comforter, but 5 inches longer.

Finish one short end of each sheet with narrow hems, and turn under 5 inches along the finished edge of the longer fabric piece. Then, with right sides together and finished edges at the same end, pin the two sheets together so that the raw edges match.

Stitch along the three unfinished edges and turn the cover right side out. Slip the cover over the comforter, tuck the long end to the inside, and fluff the duvet into a billow of comfort.

QUILTS AND COVERLETS

Patchwork quilts are the most traditional of American bedcoverings, but they don't have to be made in traditional ways. Updated versions of the classic quilt, the two coverlets shown on these pages are made by two contemporary and practical methods of construction: pillow and string quilting.

Sizing up the situation

It's easy to custom-fit either of these quilts to your bed just by adjusting the size or number of the blocks you make. But first you must measure the length and width of your mattress and decide whether the quilt should reach the floor or just clear the top of a dust ruffle.

If, for example, you decide you want a 10-inch drop on each side of the bed, add 10 inches to the foot and each side of your quilt.

To allow enough quilt at the headboard to tuck under and go over the pillows, add 12 inches to the top end. Then add 4 inches to each side of your quilt to allow for shrinkage caused by quilting. These allowances for the sides and ends are standard measurements for all quilts.

By working with the desired finished measurements of the quilt, you can decide the number of blocks you'll need and the block size. For instance, for an 80x100-inch quilt, you could make ten rows of eight 10-inch blocks.

Building a Log Cabin

The colorful quilt shown *at left* is an updated version of the traditional Log Cabin design. It's made with strips of fabric sewn diagonally into blocks, which are set together to form the diamond pattern.

To make the quilt, you'll need assorted cotton fabrics in colors of your choice, fabric

for the back of the quilt, and quilt batting to fit.

First determine the dimensions of your blocks and draw a block pattern on graph paper. Then draw several evenly spaced diagonal lines across the block. These lines will delineate your diagonal strips. Cut the paper pattern strips apart and trace around them onto cardboard, adding ¼-inch seam allowances for each side.

Cut out the cardboard templates and trace around them onto selected fabrics. When choosing fabrics, remember that the center strip in each block should be white or some other light or bright color; it is this strip that defines the diamond shapes when the blocks are joined.

Machine-stitch together the strips in each block. Then, when all the blocks are completed, lay them out on the floor and arrange them in a pleasing color pattern. Be sure to position the blocks so the direction of the strips alternates, forming diamond shapes with the center strips. Sew together all the blocks in each row, then sew the rows together.

To assemble the quilt, pin or stretch the quilt top over a layer of batting and the backing fabric. Quilt along all seam lines, then bind the edges with purchased binding.

Making a quilt from "pillows"

The puffy comforter pictured *at right* is made from miniature pillows, each stuffed with polyester fiberfill. Refer to your finished quilt dimensions to determine the number of pillows you'll need. They should all be exactly the same size, from 3 to 5 inches square.

To make each pillow, cut a rectangle of fabric the width

and twice the length of the planned pillow, adding a ¼-inch seam allowance on each side. For example, for a 4-inch square pillow, cut 4½x8½-inch rectangles.

Fold the fabric in half widthwise, right sides together, and stitch along the edges, leaving an opening on one side for turning. Clip the corners and turn the fabric, working to make the corners square.

Stuff the pillow with fiberfill. Then turn under the raw edges along the opening and stitch the pillow closed. Do the same for all the pillows in the quilt.

To assemble the quilt, lay the pillows on the floor in an attractive arrangement. Then join the pillows by overlapping adjoining edges ⅜ inch and slip-stitching across the top surface. For strength, turn the quilt over and stitch the pillows together again on the back.

CHOOSING BATTING

Quilt battings of polyester or cotton are coated with sizing for easy handling. They're machine washable and clothes-dryer safe, too.

Polyester batting holds together well; cotton battings are lightweight, but some shred easily.

With cotton battings, rows of quilting must be spaced about an inch apart, as opposed to 4 inches for polyester.

An alternative to batting is a cotton sheet blanket. Because it's woven, a cotton sheet blanket won't shred or shift, which makes it perfect for tied or sparsely stitched quilts.

QUILTS AND COVERLETS
(continued)

Tailored bedcoverings like the ones shown here look just right in a trim, uncluttered bedroom. Each spread is cut to closely surround the mattress it covers, creating a smooth, fitted appearance.

The fitted bedspread shown *at right* hangs straight from the top of the mattress. The treatment pictured *opposite* covers the mattress like a fitted sheet, and a separate skirt falls in corner pleats to the floor.

Cover your bed with style

To make either of the fitted spreads shown here, choose wool flannel, prequilted fabric, or other durable material.

Both of the spreads can cover your mattress directly and be used as a bottom sheet, in which case you'll want to use a duvet on top of the spread for warmth. Or, the spreads can cover sheets and blankets just like a regular bedspread.

For the spread *at right,* measure the mattress alone, or with all its bedcovers. Then cut pieces of fabric for the top and each of the four sides, adding ½ inch around each piece for seam allowances. (To tuck the bottom of the spread under the mattress for a fitted look, add 6 inches in width to each of the side pieces.)

Using a zipper foot, baste purchased piping (or cable cord that's covered in fabric to match the spread) to the top piece of the fitted spread. The cording should lie just inside the seam lines.

Join the bedspread side pieces along the short ends. Then stitch the sides to the bedspread top, sewing close to the piping. Trim the seams and corners, and narrow-hem the bottom of the spread.

The mattress cover shown *opposite* is made essentially the same way as the one pic-

tured *above,* except that elastic stitched in the corners gathers the bedspread around the mattress like a fitted sheet.

Follow the preceding instructions for measuring the mattress and cutting the pieces, except add a 2½-inch seam allowance to the bottom of all side pieces.

Stitch the four side pieces together, then stitch them to the top. Narrow-hem the bottom edges and stitch an 18-inch length of elastic into each corner near the hem.

For a special finishing touch, top your fitted spread with matching pillows. Instructions for making appealing pillows like the bolsters pictured *above* or the knife-edged cushions shown *opposite* appear on page 104.

Custom-tailoring a bedskirt

To make a tailored bedskirt, such as the one shown *opposite,* first construct the top of the skirt by cutting a piece of muslin the size of the top of the box spring, adding seam allowances.

Next, measure the distance from the top of the spring to the floor and cut three pieces of good-quality fabric for the pleated skirt. Dimensions for two of the pieces should be the amount of the drop by the length of the bed, plus 12 inches; the other one should be the drop by the width of the bed, plus 8 inches.

Join these three sections with ½-inch seams and hem the lower edge. Fold the corners into 4-inch-deep pleats so that the seams joining the skirt

sections fall at the back of the pleats. Pin the pleats in place.

Check the fit by placing the skirt's top on the box spring. Be sure that the seam allowances extend beyond the edges of the bed. To ensure a proper fit, round the corners of the skirt top to match the curve of the spring.

Pin the pleated skirt to the top along the sides and the foot to check the fit. Adjust the depth of the pleats so that they open exactly at the corners, then remove the skirt and press the pleats. Baste along the top of the skirt to secure the pleats in place.

Pin the skirt to the top with right sides together, easing around the corners. Stitch the skirt to the top, then hem the headboard edge.

QUILTS AND COVERLETS

(continued)

There are few quicker or easier ways to cover your bed in homemade beauty than to stitch a striking coverlet. Because the coverlet is made of sheets, no piecing is necessary. Just choose sheets that fit your bed, layer them with quilt batting, stitch, and finish.

First, measure your bed to determine the finished dimensions of the coverlet. Customarily, coverlets have a 10-inch drop on each side so that they fall about 4 inches below the mattress.

Buy two flat sheets large enough to accommodate your bed's measurements. Since you will be finishing the edges with bias binding, you don't need to worry about extra fabric for seam allowances. However, do allow about 4 inches more for both width and length for the take-up caused by quilting.

Preshrink the sheets
Preshrink your sheets in the washing machine before beginning your coverlet. Though the shrinkage will be minimal, it could be enough to cause buckling in a finished coverlet that was not preshrunk. It's a good idea to get the shrinkage out of the way before you stitch.

To assemble the coverlet, lay one preshrunk sheet face-down on the floor. On top of the sheet, lay the proper-size layer of quilt batting and then the other sheet, right side up. Using long florists' pins to accommodate the bulk, pin the three layers together. Then baste them together in horizontal and vertical rows about 4 inches apart.

Quick quilting
Now decide how you want to quilt the three layers together. You can machine-stitch them,

using straight lines to form a pattern of diamonds or squares, or you can stitch along lines dictated by the pattern in your sheet. In the coverlet pictured *at right,* for example, the sheet design suggests quilting in squares starting from the center and working toward the edges.

However you decide to quilt, you should stitch about every 4 inches to keep the batting from shifting when you wash the coverlet.

Once you've selected your quilting pattern, mark the quilting lines with a water-erasable transfer pen, available at fabric and craft stores. (When you've finished stitching, you can remove the blue lines by spraying them with cold water.)

To support all the fabric while you're stitching, surround your sewing machine with card tables. Set your machine at six to eight stitches per inch and slightly loosen the tension and pressure. Check to see that the upper and lower threads lock in the middle of the coverlet layers.

To avoid a sense of drowning in all the yardage, roll the coverlet crosswise to the center and place the roll under the arm of the sewing machine. Working from the center to the edges, stitch along your quilting lines, guiding the fabric gently and stitching at a slow, even speed.

When you've stitched half of the coverlet, remove it from the machine, roll up the completed area, unroll the remainder, and complete the quilting. Then remove the basting threads and make a fancy finish by binding the raw edges of the coverlet with bias binding or fabric strips in a coordinating color.

YARDAGE FROM SHEETS

Sheets got their start in the bedroom, so it's only fitting that they've broken into the big time in bedroom decorating schemes. When you buy sheets for sewing instead of sleeping, it's helpful to know the amount of yardage you can expect from sheets of different sizes.

With sheets that are self-hemmed, you can open the hem and gain a bit of extra yardage. Other sheets are hemmed with contrasting fabric, which cuts down on the yardage of the actual sheet fabric.

Generally, the dimensions of flat sheets with a self hem are as follows: twin, 66x104 inches; full or double, 81x104 inches; queen, 90x110 inches; and king, 108x110 inches.

For all sheets with attached hems, figure that you'll lose about 10 inches in length. Those measurements, converted to standard fabric widths, are as follows: A twin-size flat sheet will equal 4 yards of 44/45-inch-wide fabric, or 3⅛ yards of 58/60-inch-wide fabric. For a full-size sheet, the respective yardages are 4⅜ and 3⅞. For a queen-size sheet, the yardages are 5⅞ and 4½. And for a king-size sheet, the yardages are 7 yards and 5⅜ yards.

BED CURTAINS AND CANOPIES

In the days before central heating, bed curtains were a practical protection against cold drafts. Now the coziness of side curtains adds a sense of luxury to any bedroom. But achieving the effect you want needn't be extravagant—in time or expense.

The setting shown here, for example, is strictly a one-day project. Shiny brass hardware creates the four-poster effect. And for the curtains, decorator sheets come to the rescue, so there's little or no sewing.

To begin, decide the height you want the curtains to hang. This will determine the size of sheets you'll need and the length of the float rods that suspend the rails for the curtains. Measure the distance from the ceiling to the horizontal rods, the distance from the rods to the floor, and the length and width of your bed. Now, with dimensions in hand, you're ready to shop.

Finding the top brass
Your first stop is the department store to select the decorator sheets. Buy flat sheets that are long enough to reach from the curtain rods to the floor, and buy enough of them that their combined width will reach around three sides of the bed.

Now check in at the drapery department to buy three adjustable ¾-inch-diameter brass drapery rods for the wraparound rail. Two of the rods should extend the length of your bed, and the other should extend the width of it. Also pick up an ample supply of brass cafe-curtain clip-on rings, two brass sockets to fit the curtain rods, and four brass swivel joints with ¼-inch-diameter holes through the center.

Your next stop is the plumbing supply store. Here you

need to buy two pieces of brass float rod. The rods should be cut to the length you want the curtain rods to hang from the ceiling. Have the rods threaded 3 inches on each end. Also purchase two 1¼-inch brass slip nuts (designed for drainpipe fittings), two ¼ x 1½-inch brass washers, two ¼-inch brass nuts and two ¼-inch brass cap nuts. At a hardware store, pick up two butterfly nuts for ¼-inch toggle bolts.

Back at home, begin assembling the rods by drilling holes in the ceiling for the butterfly nuts. First thread a nut onto one end of each rod and drop a washer on top of it and a slip nut on top of the washer. Then screw the butterfly nuts to the float rods and insert them into the ceiling holes.

Attach the swivel joints to the rods and cap the ends with brass cap nuts. Then screw the brass sockets into the wall.

Hem the sheets, if necessary, then pinch them into pleats at 5-inch intervals and attach the cafe-curtain clips. Fasten the two outer prongs to the front of the sheet and the middle prong to the back. Finally, slip the curtain rings over the rods, and insert the rods into the rest of the hardware.

CREATE A CANOPY

To make a canopy cover, measure the width and length of your canopy frame. For the canopy ''ceiling,'' piece together a fabric rectangle that is 1 inch wider and 1 inch longer than the frame.

Cut a ruffle that is the desired height plus 2 inches and 2½ times the perimeter of the canopy. Cut a matching strip and face the ruffle. Join the two short ends to form one continuous circle and finish the other long edge.

Stitch shirring tape to one edge of the ruffle and pull up the cords in the tape until it fits around the ceiling. Leaving corners open, stitch the wrong side of the ruffle to the right side of the ceiling fabric.

Lay the canopy on the frame. Pull the shirring to fit and topstitch the ruffle corners to the ceiling fabric.

WINDOW TREATMENTS

Draperies can soften the harsh lines of a bedroom's window frames, add privacy to your room, and lend yet another coordinated touch of color and pattern to your decorating scheme. From a host of window treatments available, you might choose the formal look of the pleated draperies shown *at left,* or the more casual shirred curtains shown *opposite.*

Pinching and pleating

To begin your drapery project, first take accurate measurements of your windows *after* the hardware is installed. Measure from the rod to the sill, the apron, or the floor, depending on the length you want. Then add 7 inches to allow for the hem and heading.

To determine the width of each of the two drapery panels you'll need for your window, measure half of the length of

CREATE A CORNICE

One striking element of the window treatment pictured *at left* is the cornice, the rectangular unit above the draperies.

A cornice should be about 10 inches high, extend 6 inches from the walls, and be long enough to clear your window frame.

Cut the top, front, and two short sides from ½-inch plywood. Nail the front piece to the sides, and attach the top.

Pad the cornice with quilt batting and cover it with fabric. Then hang the cornice from metal angles attached to the sides of the window.

the rod, including the portion that curves around the corner to the wall, and double that measurement for fullness. Add an inch for finishing each side of the panels. Multiply the length by the width and convert the inches to yards.

Pleated draperies require time and effort to make, so choose a fabric that's worthy of the project. Study fiber content for resistance to fading and wrinkling, draping ability, and the method of cleaning. For a lining, polished cotton is the best buy.

To cut the fabric into panels, lay it flat and cut on the straight grain. Cut the lining panels so they are 3½ inches shorter and 6 inches narrower than the drapery panels.

Using a long, loose machine stitch, finish the bottom edges of the panels with 3-inch double hems and the lining panels with 2-inch double hems.

Join the lining and drapery panels by placing the two right sides together, with top and right-hand edges even. The lining hem should be 1½ inches above the drapery hem. Using a ¼-inch seam allowance, stitch along the right-hand edge, stopping at the top of the lining hem. Pin and stitch the left-hand edges together in the same manner. (Remember that the lining was cut narrower than the drapery fabric, so don't panic when the drapery fabric doesn't lie flat.) Turn the panel right side out.

Center the lining on the drapery by folding over the drapery edges about 3 inches on each side. Baste across the top edge.

Lay a length of pleating tape along the top edge of the drapery fabric. The pocket openings should face up, and the tape should overlap the drapery fabric about ½ inch at each side.

Sew the tape ¼ inch from the edge. Then turn the drapery fabric over and fold back the tape so it's against the lining fabric. Allow a ½-inch margin between the top of the pleater tape and the top fold of the drapery panel. Fold under the sides of the tape and stitch it to the lining over the bottom edge of the tape.

Next place one hook in each end of the drapery panel. Spacing the pleats every 4 to 6 inches, fold the centers of the pleats and pin them in place. On the right side of the drapery fabric, stitch from the top edge to the bottom edge of the tape along the pleat. Insert remaining hooks.

To complete your professional window treatment, attach drapery weights to the corners of the hem, then hang the draperies in place.

Shirred curtains

Curtains gathered or shirred on the rod are among the easiest to make. As with pleated draperies, you should first install the hardware—in this case, an expandable rod—then measure from the bottom of the rod to the apron, sill, or floor, as desired. Add 9 inches in length for casings and hem.

Multiply the width of the window by 2½, and add 4 inches for finishing. This is the width of the fabric panels for the entire window, so now divide by two to figure the width of each of two panels.

Hem the sides of the panels, and form the top casing by folding over the edge and stitching. Slip the rod through the casing and hang the curtain. Then pin up the hem, remove the curtain from the rod, and hem the bottom.

TOP A TABLE

Full-length round table-cloths like the white one pictured *above* can beautify any table.

Measure the diameter of your tabletop and add twice the height of the table and 1 inch for the hem. This equals the total tablecloth diameter.

If the diameter is less than 65 inches, use a twin sheet; up to 80 inches, use a double; up to 89 inches, use a queen; and up to 99 inches, use a king.

Cut out the circle, hem the edge, and drape over the table.

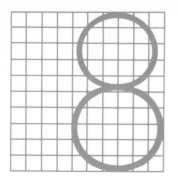

AMENITIES

A bedroom amenity can be as simple as a rocking chair, as romantic as a private balcony, or as up-to-the-minute as a spa. It all depends on how you define relaxation, how much and what kind of space is available, and, most of all, your overall taste and preferences. Let this chapter show you how to take advantage of extra features your bedroom already offers, and how to create them if they're not yet there.

ROOMS WITH A VIEW

There's nothing more inviting than a room with a view. If an appealing vista is beckoning beyond your bedroom windows, don't hide it behind elaborate draperies. The best way to play up your view is to play down your window treatments; this is no place for busily patterned fabrics, fussy cornices, or distracting swags.

Instead, choose clean and simple alternatives. Mini-slat and vertical blinds often are ideal. They can be raised or drawn to the side to clear the windows completely; you also can tilt them to block the sun and provide partial privacy without losing your view or blocking incoming breezes. Other possibilities include roll-up or Roman shades or louvered shutters.

A view can set the tone for your decorating scheme, too. Consider keying colors and materials to what lies beyond the windows. In the bedroom pictured here, earth tones and natural woods and baskets set a restful mood that's in keeping with the countryside beyond. The undraped windows and high vaulted ceiling enchance the airy feeling of spaciousness suggested by the treetop view.

A flower-brightened deck, abundant garden, or dramatic cityscape deserves attention. Try moving the bed to take full advantage of such a view, as shown *at right*. If reading and lounging are top priorities, position your favorite chair, chaise, or floor pillows near the window.

THE WARMTH OF A FIREPLACE

The golden glow of flames, the pleasant crackle of burning wood, and the warmth of a fire are magic in any room and especially appealing in a master bedroom. Even in summer, with plants or flowers brightening the hearth, a fireplace is an eye-appealing focal point. If you're fortunate enough to have a bedroom fireplace, by all means play it up as the decorative asset it is. If your bedroom doesn't have a fireplace and you've always wanted one, read on.

In the welcoming bedroom pictured *at right,* flickering flames and warm red walls set a mood that's both cozy and elegant. To emphasize the room's major attraction, the owners painted the mantel white and surrounded the fireplace opening with white tiles. A nubby rug, a handwoven coverlet, an antique quilt, and decades-old wood pieces add their own special appeal.

One good way to call attention to a richly detailed fireplace like this one is with contrast. If your walls are light in color, consider painting the fireplace a dark color. Pick up a color from nearby artwork or other accessories, or from your sheets or bedspread. Or play up the grain of a natural wood mantel by surrounding it with crisp white walls.

Because a fireplace is the focal point in almost any room that has one, you'll probably want to avoid other features that visually compete with it. Here, for example, simple

white mini-slat blinds provide privacy without hiding the beautiful window trim or diverting attention from the fireplace.

Gather furnishings around the fire

To make the most of a bedroom fireplace, position the bed so you can enjoy the glow until you fall asleep. If you have room, make even more of your fireplace by placing seating pieces near it. A small table and a rocker or a lounge chair may be all you need to turn a few square feet into a fireside sitting spot. In the bedroom shown here, an upholstered love seat invites cozy lounging, and an easy-care plastic cocktail table holds drinks and snacks. If you plan nocturnal reading in your sitting spot, add a floor lamp, a small table lamp, or a wall-mounted flex-arm light next to your chair or sofa.

If you don't already have a bedroom fireplace, you may be able to add one. Freestanding fireplaces and prefab built-in models can be installed more easily than you might think. You need a flue, of course, but you needn't go to the bother of building an expensive masonry chimney. Insulated metal flues can go up through the ceiling and roof or up an exterior wall.

How much space does a fireplace require? Fire codes vary, but generally freestanding units must rest on a noncombustible base that extends 18 inches from the front and sides of the fireplace and a minimum of 36 inches from the back. Built-in "zero-clearance" units can be entirely or partly recessed into a wall; usually they must be fronted with a noncombustible hearth that is at least 16 inches wider than the fireplace opening and at least 16 inches deep.

SAFETY AND EFFICIENCY

In a bedroom, an open firebox is almost as dangerous as smoking in bed. Furthermore, an unsealed opening wastes energy. While the fire is burning, it consumes household air you've already paid to heat; when the fire goes out, warm room air continues going up the chimney.

The solution to these problems is to seal the opening with fireproof glass doors that can be opened for the warmth of the fire and closed before you retire.

SPECIAL LIGHTING EFFECTS

After sundown, creative lighting can turn an ordinary bedroom into a special place. Work spaces, such as kitchens, need bright and even illumination, but lighting in bedrooms can be subtle and decorative. Picture a single spotlight piercing a dark stage, and you'll begin to realize the dramatic potential inherent in light. A flexible bedroom plan includes soft, adjustable, ambient lighting; task lighting for reading or desk work; and accent lighting for special effects.

The lighting design in the bedroom pictured here creates a futuristic mood. The bed itself seems to float in the room, thanks to a string of inexpensive low-voltage bulbs hung from hooks screwed into the bed's double-deck platform, shown *at upper right.* The same kind of lighting also runs beneath the window seat pictured *at lower right.* A canister uplight placed on top of the freestanding storage unit in the photograph *opposite* bounces light off the ceiling. Soft illumination, combined with an all-gray color scheme, blurs the borders between walls, ceiling, and floor for an effect of limitless space. Two adjustable bedside lamps serve late-night readers.

Low-voltage, energy-efficient lighting isn't restricted to the Christmas-tree type of lights used in this bedroom. After plugging in a 6- or 12-volt transformer to step down the household voltage from 120 volts, you can add low-voltage track or recessed lighting to provide pinpoint spots or larger pools of light. You can direct a beam to highlight a plant or favorite artwork, or subtly brighten the corners of the room by aiming downlights from the ceiling or uplights from the floor. A pair of 25-watt, adjustable, low-voltage track fixtures over the bed can provide reading lights.

Other options

For soft general illumination, consider cove or soffit lighting. In a cove setup the housing is open at the top and light is reflected off the ceiling. Soffit lighting directs light down. The light source in both systems is concealed and glare-free. Use incandescent lamps or warm-white fluorescents that flatter skin tones; a dimmer switch lets you fine-tune the system.

DESIGN FOR SIGHT AND SOUND

Sophisticated television and audio equipment expands our world of sight and sound. But where, in a small home, can you steal away for a while and find uninterrupted time to soothe your eyes and ears? For many parents, the master bedroom already is an entertainment center of sorts, with a TV set positioned within sight of the bed. Bring a stereo system in there, too, then plan the room as a welcoming place where you can shut out the world, put your feet up, look, and listen.

For your bedroom to become a spot for lounging, reading, listening to music, watching television, or simply thinking, you don't need a lot of furnishings. In fact, a sight-and-sound sanctuary calls for simplicity—quiet background colors, clean lines, a minimum of clutter, and, of course, comfort. In addition to a bed, chair, or sofa that invites lounging, the key ingredients are locations to place and plug in equipment.

In the bedroom pictured *at right,* built-in shelves and storage drawers eliminate the need for other furniture. The television set pulls out on a special shelf and swivels for comfortable viewing from the bed. Home video and stereo equipment is neatly tucked away behind the doors, with speakers (not shown) strategically located on the opposite side of the room. Recessed overhead lighting, controlled with a dimmer switch, washes the walls with soft lighting.

Plain-textured, neutral-toned walls and carpet like those shown here make an ideally soothing background. This kind of backdrop has a "clean-slate" look that makes it easier to concentrate on sights and sounds, rather than on the surroundings.

In the bedroom pictured here, the homeowners introduced a touch of color and pattern by adding a comforter and bed skirt made of a subtly patterned fabric.

Keep in mind that textures add more than eye appeal and comfort. Nubby carpet, soft upholstery, and the sink-in softness of a quilted comforter are inviting touches that also do a lot for the acoustical quality of a room. That's especially important when you want good sound that won't disturb the rest of the family.

AN ENTIRE MASTER WING

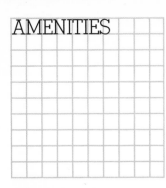

If your home is large enough and your children old enough, you may decide the time has come for you to have an entire master wing—your own home-within-a-home. Often an overlooked attic can be remodeled into a lofty, private, and peaceful parents' retreat. Or you may be planning an addition to your house and think of an apartment-size suite as the ultimate bedroom amenity. Let the comfortable quarters shown here inspire you to create your haven.

The two-room suite pictured on these pages was created by two processes: First, an existing bedroom was converted into a sitting room, and then a 10x19-foot bedroom was added on. Whether you already have ample space or are simply in the planning stages of adding on, many of the ideas these homeowners implemented can find a home in your house, too.

If you're planning a master suite, you'll probably want to rely on color and pattern to tie the spaces together—not necessarily the same colors or patterns, but related ones that work well together to provide variety without sharp contrast. In the bedroom pictured *at upper left* and the sitting room pictured *opposite,* the same floral fabric is used in several places: for curtains, for an ottoman and chair in the sitting room, and for the draperies and bedspread. Accessories in both areas emphasize the shared color scheme.

Although a master wing should be welcoming and homey, you may not consider clutter to be the key to coziness. Here, built-ins unclutter this master suite. Along one wall of the sitting room, the former bedroom closet was turned into a vanity/dressing table, shown *at lower left.* Handsome panel doors close the dressing table off from view when it's not in use. Opposite the fireplace wall in the sitting room (out of camera range), a wall of storage drawers, shelves, and space for hanging clothes was built.

The former exterior brick became the focal point of the sitting room. A fireplace, visible from both the sitting and sleeping areas, was added for both charm and practical warmth.

REMOVING WALLS FOR A WIDE-OPEN LOOK

A room without walls isn't as revolutionary as it may sound. First, there was the open-plan kitchen, with counters and pass-throughs and the opportunity to talk with family and friends while preparing a meal. Then the concept expanded to merge family and informal dining areas. An open plan in sleeping quarters represents a natural progression from more public places in a home; this concept makes particular sense in master bedrooms, where ambience and a sense of space are so important.

If your idea of luxury is lots of space around you, the best way to achieve that may be to remove all or part of a wall or walls. When you plan your master suite, rely on low partitions instead of floor-to-ceiling walls to divide without a cut-up feeling.

The free-flowing master suite pictured *at right* is a good example of thoughtful, open-plan remodeling. Two small bedrooms and a bath were combined to create sleeping, bathing, dressing, and vanity areas. Because ordinary walls would have created a dark, warrenlike feeling in this relatively small space, storage units are used to subtly separate the areas.

The color scheme contributes to the airy, spacious feeling, too. The soft beige walls and carpet are neutral and blend with each other to keep the open look alive. Colorful bed linens provide easily varied accents.

A new skylight located above the central storage core provides light where it's needed most; because the partitions are low, the added light benefits virtually all corners of the suite. Boxed-in fluorescent tubes positioned at strategic intervals give additional light wherever it's needed. Judiciously placed mirror panels expand apparent space and aid in dressing. Out of view and around the corner from the bed, a vanity and partitioned toilet efficiently line up along one wall; a new combination shower/soaking tub occupies another corner.

GUEST QUARTERS

These days, having a room set aside for the exclusive use of guests is an amenity in itself. But even if your guest room is a home office, den, or multipurpose storage place most of the time, you'd probably like it to be a gracious home-away-from-home for guests when they arrive. Soothing colors, attractive furnishings and accessories, and a small closet to call their own will make guests feel welcome and comfortable.

The attractive and efficient room shown on these two pages performs well as both a guest room and a den. A custom-made, carpeted sleeping platform occupies the center of the room and doubles as an everyday seating unit. Behind the backrest, a Parsons table serves as both desk and night table. An acrylic trunk nestled beneath the table holds extra bed linens; a lamp on top of the table illumi-

nates both the desk and the bed. Beige carpeting and walls set a warm, peaceful mood for the room. To avoid a closed-in feeling in this modest-size space, mirrors cover one wall. Mini-slat blinds, less obtrusive than bulky draperies, add privacy for guests.

Storage for guests' belongings is a basic need in any guest room. The room shown

here provides ample surface space and storage in the cabinets next to the fireplace and the closet on the mirrored wall.

Even if your guest room is solely a guest room and doesn't also serve for family activities, multipurpose furnishings add convenience. A daybed, sleep sofa, or flip-open chair that converts to a bed can be a comfort for a guest who wants a private sitting place during the day.

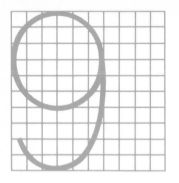

BEDROOM PROJECTS YOU CAN BUILD

Make your bed. No, forget about smoothing out the sheets and plumping up the pillows. We mean build your bed. Compared to making other kinds of furniture, building beds is relatively easy for a handy do-it-yourselfer. This chapter presents a sleeper's choice of projects, including a crib, island bed, Murphy bed, bunk bed, platform bed, and water bed frame. You can build any of these projects as shown or add your own custom touches.

A SEE-THROUGH CRIB

Building a project similar to the one on the opposite page isn't exactly child's play, but once you've got it together, this crib will be a stylishly useful addition to your home's nursery. Transparent acrylic panels at the head and foot let baby get a good view outside, and also make it easier to check on the baby no matter how the crib is placed in the room.

Our version is made of oak. You might prefer to use maple or clear pine, or a less expensive grade of pine if you plan to paint the crib.

To begin the job, construct a bed frame by butt-joining 1x4s, as shown in the drawing *below*. Then screw 1x2 ledger strips on the inner sides of the frame and install a piece of ½-inch plywood to support the mattress.

Use 1x2s and ¾x1-inch slats for the sides, mortising the joints to ensure that your work is as strong as possible. As you're spacing the slats, place them no more than 2⅜ inches apart so the baby's head can't get caught. A pair of window spring bolts and metal guide pins let you raise and lower one side. The pins and spring bolts slide up and down in tracks you rout into the two legs.

Make the legs and top rails from 1x4s, with rabbet joints where they meet. With a router, make dado cuts for the tracks and the acrylic panels. Drill two holes into each leg—one near the top and one at mattress level—for the spring bolts to latch into.

Attach the legs to the bed frame with screws. A second set of screw holes lower on the legs lets you lower the mattress and bed frame when baby is bigger.

Using dowel joints, fasten the stationary side to the legs. Position the movable side between the legs containing the routed track.

Sand all the pieces and apply a hard finish such as polyurethane or high-gloss paint. Make sure the finish you choose is nontoxic and contains no lead.

Finally, drop the acrylic panels into place, and complete the project by nailing and gluing the top rails to the legs.

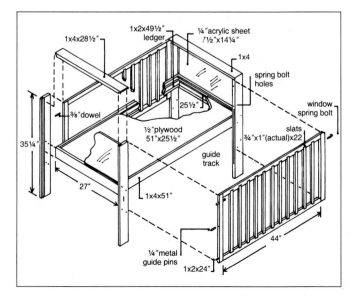

AN ISLAND BED

Instead of exiling your bed to a corner or shoving it against a wall, make it the center of attention. Built from plywood and 1x12s, the handsomely carpeted, freestanding bed shown in the photo has a self-contained electrical system that helps transform an ordinary mattress and spring set into a multipurpose entertainment center. Easy to assemble, it's a perfect place to catch up on bedtime reading, chat long-distance with far-away friends, or relax to soft, late-night music.

With the mattress and springs on the floor, use 1x12s to construct a three-sided, U-shaped frame around both sides and the foot of the bed. Butt-join all edges, gluing and nailing them in place.

To build the bookcase headboard, use ¾-inch plywood. Cut the large front member to accept a box of 1x12s, as illustrated in the drawing *below*. Then butt-join the plywood pieces together.

Nail 1x2 ledger strips to the headboard, and attach the frame, as shown.
Install electrical outlets near the top of each side. Drill two holes for the lamps and install a jack for the telephone.

Installing the carpet cover-up is a tricky job. If you're careful and unusually patient, you can do the job yourself, using glue and a heavy-duty staple gun. However, if you're not sure you can negotiate tricky corners with a minimum of slip-ups, it may be better to hire a professional carpet installer.

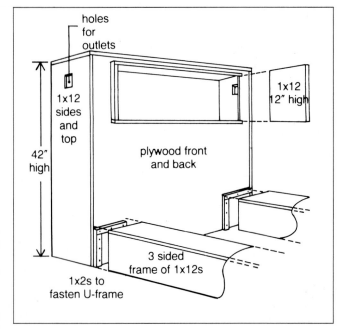

holes for outlets

42" high

1x12 sides and top

1x12 12" high

plywood front and back

3 sided frame of 1x12s

1x2s to fasten U-frame

A MURPHY BED

In a home where space is tight and rooms must have multiple personalities, a fold-down Murphy bed could be just what the decorator ordered. When the bed is up and out of sight, you can use the room as daytime living space. Flip the bed down and the area suddenly becomes an ideal guest room or even an extra full-time bedroom. The thoroughly modern Murphy bed shown here has two more things going for it: a flip-down table that doubles as a wall decoration when it's in the up position. Everything goes together with plywood and other ordinary building materials, a few piano hinges, and brick or sand ballast. The ballast counterbalances the bed's weight so you can easily lift and lower it.

Begin by building the bed itself with 2x4s, ½-inch plywood, and dimension lumber, as shown in the large drawing *below*. Then, using 1x6s, assemble a ballast box and attach it to the front of the bed. Later you'll fill the box with bricks, sandbags, or other heavy material to counterbalance the bed. Measure the depth of the box carefully; it must be shallow enough to clear the wall when the bed pivots.

When the bed is lowered it rests on a single piano-hinged support that folds flat against the bottom. The bed support detail inset *at lower left* in the drawing shows how this feature works.

Build the enclosure with 2x4 studs and sheathe it with drywall. Remember to leave clearances as you go along: ¼ inch on either side, ½ inch at the bottom, and at least 1 inch at the top.

Put the bed in place by standing it in the closed position on a ½-inch-thick piece of scrap lumber. Then slide the entire unit so the front edge is recessed about ½ inch into the enclosure. Drill holes and insert bushings and lag screws through the bed frame into the side of the enclosure, as shown in the pivot detail drawing. If the bed doesn't pivot smoothly, redrill and relocate the hardware.

When you're satisfied with the pivoting action, raise the bed. Drill holes through each side of the bed frame into the 2x4 framing. These accommodate removable ½-inch dowels that secure the bed when it's not in use.

The table consists of two pieces of ¾-inch plywood hinged to each other and to the bottom of the bed, as shown in the tabletop detail *at upper right* of the drawing.

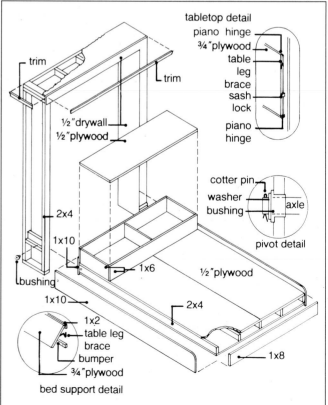

tabletop detail

piano hinge
¾"plywood
table
leg
brace
sash
lock
piano
hinge

trim

trim

½"drywall
½"plywood

2x4

1x10

bushing

1x10

cotter pin
washer
bushing
axle

pivot detail

1x6

½"plywood

2x4

1x2
table leg
brace
bumper
¾"plywood

1x8

bed support detail

A BUNK BED

When two kids share a bedroom, you can forget about elegant furnishings and fancy accoutrements. What you need most are solid pieces that stand up to hard knocks, sticky fingers, and children's roughhousing. The easily built bunk bed shown here may be just the tough customer you're after. Made of plywood and covered with plastic laminate, it's difficult to chip or scuff yet simple to keep clean. In addition, the money saved building it on your own can be used to buy or build equally sturdy bedroom furniture such as the desk shown in the foreground of our photo.

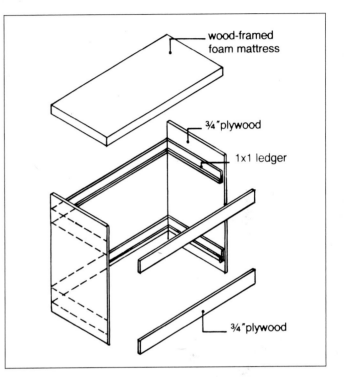

S tart by measuring the width, length, and depth of the mattresses you're going to use. For this project, the wood-framed foam variety will work best. These have their own solid bottoms; if you decide to use ordinary mattresses, you'll need to include ¾-inch plywood panels for the mattresses to rest on.

With your dimensions as a guide, build both box frames from ¾-inch plywood, as shown in the drawing *above*. Butt-join the edges so the longer sides overlap the shorter ones; this way you won't see the joints when the end panels are added. Glue and nail the joints together and screw 1x1 ledger strips to the frames, as illustrated.

Cut the supporting end panels from ¾-inch plywood. Where you decide to attach the box frames will depend on the depth of the mattresses and how high you want the beds to be.

Then, beginning with the lower box, secure the frames to the end panels, countersinking the screws as you go. To hold the boxes in position while you work, temporarily nail ledger strips to the end panels and rest the boxes on them. Remove these ledger strips when the unit is screwed together.

Complete the job with the finish of your choice. This project is covered with durable plastic laminate, but a gloss enamel finish also will take a lot of hard knocks.

If you have room at the foot or head, you could expand this unit by building a wardrobe unit, desk, or bookcase at one end. Or dress up one of the end panels with a full-length mirror, bulletin board, or blackboard. For young children, you might want to add railings that can be removed later.

A PLATFORM BED

If you're looking for ways to furnish a house without emptying your pocketbook, the versatile project pictured here may fit your plans perfectly. At night, it's a cozy platform bed. During the day, it's an equally comfortable sofa. Day *and* night, it's also a hardworking storage unit, with bookcases on either side. Plus, the whole thing is so easy to put together, nearly any do-it-yourselfer can build it in a day.

As it is for other projects in this chapter, plywood again is the best material to work with. It's strong, free of warping and irregularities, and—for the budget-conscious builder—relatively inexpensive. You can choose plywood in a variety of surface veneers. Fir is the most common and least expensive, but birch and oak veneers also are widely available.

To begin, measure the length and width of the mattress you plan to use. These numbers will determine the length and width of the bed board and the outside width of the bookcases. The bookcases can be exactly the same width as the bed, or extend on one or both sides.

Using ¾-inch plywood, cut 10-inch-wide strips for the bed frame. Assemble the frame, butt-joining all edges with glue and nails, as shown *below*.

If you have the skills and equipment, you might prefer to use a more sophisticated joinery system. Though tricky to make, splined or doweled miters would give the bookcase units a more professional and furniture-like appearance.

To make the bookcases, cut all pieces from ¾-inch plywood. Then, as illustrated, glue and nail them together, again using simple butt joints.

So that you will be able to take apart everything easily when necessary, screw through the backs of the bookcases to the frame.

From a piece of ¾-inch plywood, cut a bed board equal in size to the mattress. If your bed will be more than 48 inches wide, you may need more than one piece of plywood; you should brace the joint between panels underneath with a double-thick length of ¾-inch plywood standing on edge. Screw the bed board or boards to the top of the frame.

Add plywood edging tape to all exposed edges. Or sand them lightly until they're smooth; then fill any voids.

To complete the job, apply one or two coats of clear sealer, varnish, or paint. Let the finish dry and top the bed off with a fabric-covered mattress or futon. For daytime lounging, add bolsters or big pillows at the ends. (To learn about making pillows, see pages 104 and 105.)

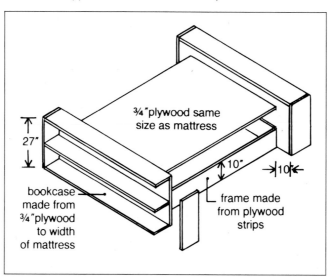

27"

¾"plywood same size as mattress

10"

10"

bookcase made from ¾"plywood to width of mattress

frame made from plywood strips

A WATER BED FRAME

Relaxing on a water bed is an almost weightless sensation. You literally float on a cushion of water that exactly molds itself to your body, with no pressure points to cut off circulation. Kids love water beds. So do pregnant women, adults with back problems, and almost everyone who'd like a mild sense of adventure in slumberland.

A water bed can be heavy—up to 2,000 pounds—but, surprisingly, it isn't the floor that has to bear the brunt of all that weight. On a per-square-foot basis, a king-size mattress of water weighs about the same as a refrigerator; however, most stresses are not on the floor but at the mattress sides, where the water inside would like to burst the seams of its vinyl container.

This means a water bed must be surrounded by a sturdy frame. Ordinary 2x12 lumber, lag-bolted at the corners, will do the job. If you'd like to contain your water bed with a more elegant enclosure, and gain storage, too, consider a project like this one. Built of ¾-inch particleboard and surfaced with stainless steel laminate, it features a pair of lift-top bedding bins on each side and open compartments for books and magazines at the foot.

This is not an easy project to construct. At two corners you need the skill and equipment to make compound miter joints; other elements require straightforward (but accurate) miters. And the entire structure must be strong enough to securely contain the mattress.

Examine the drawing *below* and you can see that the frame consists of three elongated units. Use glue and screws to assemble the components of each unit. Note that the base of the side storage bins extends just 5½ inches into the mattress area; you don't need a solid bottom beneath the entire bed. Dividers inside the bins add strength and compartmentalized storage for sheets and blankets.

Surface each unit with laminate, hang the bedding bins' doors with piano hinges, and install pulls. Then bolt the units together into a U-shape, with the open end against a wall. After leveling and squaring the frame, secure the head to the floor with wood screws.

Now install a plinth and platform inside the enclosure, cover them with a liner and the mattress, fill the mattress with water, and settle in for a serene snooze. To learn about plinths and platforms, and about choosing a water bed mattress, liner, heater, and other components, see pages 148 and 149.

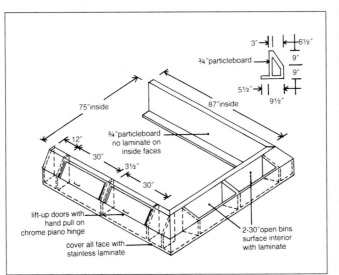

3″
6½″
¾″ particleboard
9″
9″
5½″
9½″

75″inside
87″inside

¾″ particleboard
no laminate on
inside faces

12″
30″
3½″
30″

lift-up doors with
hand pull on
chrome piano hinge

cover all face with
stainless laminate

2-30″ open bins
surface interior
with laminate

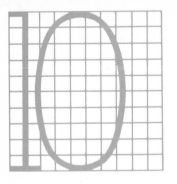

CHOOSING AND BUYING BEDROOM FURNISHINGS

Once you decide on the best room arrangement, and the number and type of furnishings you'll need, you'll want to acquire high-quality pieces that will live up to your expectations. Anyone who has faced morning after a night of tossing and turning on an uncomfortable bed knows the importance of being an informed shopper. On top of the bed, well-chosen linens will surround you with comfort as well as style. And because you'll be opening and closing many clothing drawers on a daily basis, it also is important to select sturdy bedroom storage pieces.

Walk into any bedroom with a beautifully crafted headboard, and it's probably the first thing you notice. How well a headboard plays a starring role largely depends on its good looks. Our cast of headboards shown *opposite* illustrates some of the styles available.

Handsome rattan or wicker headboards styled with straight or gently curving lines are contemporary classics that work well in informal bedrooms. Simply designed headboards made of oak or pine are other good choices.

For more formal settings, consider more traditional options. Headboards made of fine woods, such as mahogany, walnut, and cherry, are readily available in many popular styles, including Queen Anne, Chippendale, Oriental, and French. These showstoppers are graced with authentic details, but scaled for today's smaller rooms.

Brass headboards are another all-time favorite. Many made today mimic turn-of-the-century styles, but you'll also find contemporary designs with straight lines and simple finials.

For a softer, custom look, consider a padded headboard upholstered to complement your bedcoverings.

Beyond appearance

Do you like to read or breakfast in bed? Does your bed "float" in the center of the room? In any of these cases, you'll want a headboard that's functional as well as attractive. If you plan to lean your pillows against it, you'll probably prefer a fairly high headboard with a smooth, solid surface or a padded, upholstered one.

Regardless of which type you like, the quality of any headboard is based on two things: workmanship and materials. To distinguish between good and second-rate headboards, shop around and carefully examine pieces in the various price ranges. Although not all well-built headboards are expensive, cost can be one indicator of quality.

When shopping for wood headboards, look for solid wood frames, corner blocks that are screwed and glued into place, and a smooth finish that's consistent in color and glossiness.

Wicker or rattan headboards also should have sturdy frames. The frame, which can be either wood or metal, should be completely covered by woven fibers. Also check to see that weaving is even, and that the fibers are consistently colored and finished.

Solid brass and brass-plated headboards should have smooth, blemish-free surfaces and a uniform, mirrorlike gloss. If you choose a brass-plated headboard, make sure the protective lacquer finish is free of scratches or nicks. Otherwise the exposed layer of brass will tarnish.

Putting things in place

Most standard metal bed frames are made with brackets to accommodate a headboard, but with no fittings for a footboard. If you plan to use both, you'll need a double-ended frame. Other options include frame sets with integral head- and footboards, or versions with side runners that connect the head and foot.

If you're short on stowing space, consider a storage headboard. Some dual-purpose designs look like traditional bookcase headboards, but are hinged at the top to reveal storage space that goes all the way to the floor.

CHOOSING AND BUYING BEDROOM FURNISHINGS

MATTRESSES

king 76"x 80"
(California king 72"x 84")

queen 60"x 80"

double 53"x 75"
(double extra long 53"x 80")

twin 38"x 75"
(twin extra long 38"x 80")

Your bedroom is first and foremost a place to sleep, so you'll want to have a comfortable mattress. Take a few minutes to evaluate the mattress you're sleeping on now. Does it still provide firm yet resilient support, or is it lumpy and sagging in the middle? Is it large enough to provide ample sleeping space? If your old mattress has seen better days, consider retiring it and replacing it with one that will give you a good night's sleep.

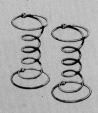

Bonnell spring

pocketed spring

continuous spring

Choosing the right size mattress depends on the size of the bedroom and the size and habits of the sleeper or sleepers. A double-size mattress shared by two people, for example, offers each only the sleeping width of a crib. The photo *at left* presents standard measurements, accepted by most bedding manufacturers, for various size mattresses.

Conventional mattresses come in two main types: innerspring and foam. For both, inner construction determines overall quality.

A standard innerspring mattress is made of rows of steel coils sandwiched between layers of insulation and cushioning material. The number of coils often is used as an indicator of quality. But what's more important is the gauge of the coil wire (the lower the gauge, the thicker the wire), the number of coil convolutions, and the way the coils work together. Generally, the thicker the wire and the more turns, the firmer the support.

Three popular spring configurations are illustrated *opposite, below*. Hourglass-shaped *Bonnell coils* are most widely used. Barrel-shaped *pocketed springs* contain each coil in its own fabric pocket. *Continuous springs* feature a connected wire network instead of individual coil springs.

Some high-quality mattresses feature stabilizer springs around the perimeter of the unit. This construction lets you comfortably lie close to the edge of the mattress.

Upholstery and ticking

What comes between you and the springs also affects the comfort of the mattress. The innermost layer of cushioning is made of coconut fiber, crimped hair, or a synthetic material. On top of this are several softer layers of cotton felt, wool, hair, or foam. Natural materials provide maximum absorption.

Mattress ticking can be made of cotton, synthetics, or a combination of materials. If you like firm support, but softness directly underneath your body, select a "soft-top" mattress with an extra-plush layer beneath the ticking.

Turning a mattress prolongs its life, so look for mattresses with handles on the sides. Many feature air holes that keep moisture from becoming trapped inside the mattress.

A matching box spring will reinforce support and extend the life of the mattress. Box spring coils may be either cone- or hourglass-shaped. Some box springs feature metal grids or torsion bars instead of coils.

A *foam mattress* has a core of cushiony plastic foam within a colorful cover. Two types of urethane foam are available—standard foam and new high-resiliency foam, which provides firmer support. The heavier the mattress, the denser the foam, and the better the support.

CHOOSING AND BUYING BEDROOM FURNISHINGS

WATER BEDS

Once considered a fad, water beds now are widely accepted alternatives to conventional mattresses. What makes them so popular? One reason is that a water bed mattress conforms to your body's shape, so support is evenly distributed and tossing and turning are minimized. Another reason is that water beds are equipped with heaters, so they're soothingly warm on cold nights. Also important to note are two new developments in water beds. The first, waveless water beds, come equipped with baffles that do away with the swaying movement of earlier models. A more recent introduction is the hybrid water bed, which is made of water compartments surrounded by sheets of foam. Hybrid mattresses can be used with standard box springs, bed frames, and bed linens.

The parts of a conventional water bed, shown *at right*, typically are sold in a package, but you also can purchase them separately.

The main component is the mattress, which is available in two styles. The less expensive kind looks like a knife-edged pillow made of two panels of vinyl joined on all four sides. Stronger, higher-quality, box-shaped mattresses feature top and bottom panels joined to separate side pieces.

How the mattress panels are joined is another indication of quality. Butt seams, in which the panels are joined edge to edge, often are found on economy mattresses. Double-lap seams are more durable.

A liner, which fits inside the frame, surrounds the mattress and catches any water that may leak out during filling or draining, or from a puncture.

Installed beneath the mattress is the heater, which is similar to a large, waterproof heating pad. Make sure the heater is Underwriters Laboratories (UL) approved; a solid-state heater will offer you optimum temperature control.

The support system for a conventional water bed consists of the frame, which cradles the mattress and liner, and the decking and pedestal, which support the frame and raise it to a comfortable height.

Conventional water beds require sheets that are specially constructed to ensure a secure fit. The top sheet is joined to the bottom sheet along the bottom edge and the bottom sheet is equipped with triangular pockets that fit snugly beneath the mattress. Specially designed mattress pads also provide a buffer between your body and the mattress. An electric pump makes filling and emptying easier.

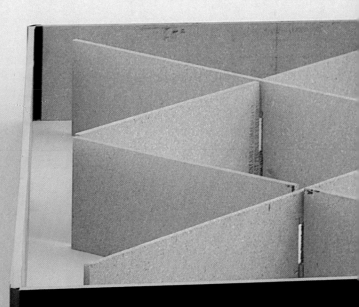

The best buys in bed-room storage pieces reward you with lots of stowing compartments without taking up too much floor space. Free-standing pieces offer the added advantage of versatility; you can rearrange them as your storage needs change, something you can't do with built-in closets or cabinets. You will want to select well-built pieces that will last as long as your ideas for using them.

Modular storage units, like the ones pictured *at left,* offer a lot of flexibility at a reasonable price. Many have adjustable shelves or bins that are easily raised or lowered. When your storage needs grow, you can add compatible pieces to stack on top or line up alongside existing units. Before you buy, make sure the units fit together snugly and stack securely.

To get the most out of modular units, make sure the backs also are finished. That way you can use them away from the walls as room dividers or in island storage arrangements. The backs of better pieces will be inset and screwed into the frame. Backs that are stapled into place are a sign of cheaper construction.

Whether you choose modular pieces or more traditional case goods, the way the drawers are constructed is a good indication of the overall quality of a piece. Look for drawers that open smoothly with center or side glides. Better units also feature stops that keep the drawer from being pulled out or pushed in too far. Avoid furniture with butt-joined drawers; this construction probably will not stand up to daily use. Dovetail joints are used in drawer construction of top-quality cases. Feel the insides of the drawers; they should be smooth and well-sanded, with no rough edges to snag clothing or linens.

One especially efficient way to increase the storage space in your bedroom is to make use of wasted space under the bed. The trundle-style bed shown *at left,* for example, puts space underneath to use for storing linens and extra pillows. Other platform beds are equipped with several smaller storage drawers.

CHOOSING AND BUYING BEDROOM FURNISHINGS

SOFT GOODS

Completing the picture of the perfect bedroom calls for eye-catching sheets, blankets, pillowcases, and comforters. Today, the choices are almost unlimited. Fashionable colors, patterns, and fabrics give the phrase "making the bed" a whole new, glamorous meaning.

Good looks may draw your eye to a sheet pattern, but it's the quality of the sheeting fabric that will make the real difference when you slip into bed. Good-quality *muslin* sheets have a thread count (the number of threads per square inch) of 128 to 130. *Percale* sheets typically have a thread count of 180 to 200; their higher thread count makes them softer, smoother, and more expensive than muslin sheets.

A blend of 50 percent cotton/50 percent polyester once was standard for sheets, but now you'll find blends of 65/35, 70/30, and 80/20. If you prefer 100 percent cotton, you can find no-iron percale versions, although they're more expensive than the synthetic combinations.

Flannel sheets keep you toasty on cold winter nights, and the flat sheets also work well as lightweight summer blankets. You'll find these soft-napped sheets in 100 percent cotton or in less expensive cotton/polyester blends.

Blankets, comforters, and duvets

When choosing blankets, you'll need to consider what they're made of as well as their warmth, weight, washability, and price.

• *Blanket*s are basically of two types—natural (wool and sometimes cotton) and synthetic. *Wool* blankets are very warm and soft to the touch, and come in a wide range of colors. Although expensive, a good wool blanket should last at least 15 years. New wool blankets usually are moth-proofed; older ones need additional storage protection. Some are machine washable; others must be dry-cleaned. Check the label for instructions. *Synthetic* blankets are less expensive than wool ones, machine washable, and nonallergenic.

Thermal blankets, usually made of acrylic, cotton, or wool, have an open waffle-weave and can be used year round. In summer they let air circulate, and in winter they trap body heat when used beneath another covering.

Flocked blankets are non-woven and are made of nylon bonded to a layer of foam. They are plush and warm and won't pill. Instead of "breathing" as a thermal or woven blanket does, flocked blankets trap air between fibers.

You'll also find inexpensive needle-punched blankets, which are made of sheets of fiber that are layered and needle-punched together. They are not as long-lasting as a woven blanket.

Electric blankets warm you with flexible heating wires hidden inside an acrylic envelope. Blankets larger than twin size are available with dual controls so each side of the blanket can be regulated separately. Thermostats embedded throughout the blanket automatically shut off electricity if it starts to overheat. Check for the Underwriters Laboratories symbol, which indicates the blanket has been tested for safety.

• *Comforters* usually are made with a decorative quilted outer shell of cotton, or a polyester/cotton blend. Sometimes they have a layer of flocked nylon or flannel on the underside. The most luxurious, warmest, and highest-priced comforters are stuffed with down. Comforters filled with lamb's wool are less costly and almost as warm and light as those filled with down, but not as easy to find. The most economical and readily available comforters are stuffed with synthetic fibers (usually polyester fiberfill). To judge the quality of these bed-coverings, squeeze them to compare density and thickness. The more filling, the fluffier and warmer the comforter.

(continued)

WHERE TO GO FOR MORE INFORMATION

SOFT GOODS
(continued)

• *Duvets* (also called continental quilts) simplify bedmaking because they take the place of top sheets, blankets, and bedspreads. Duvets are channel-quilted and usually filled with down or a combination of down and feathers. The distinctive feature of a duvet is the unquilted decorative cover that slips over it like a giant pillowcase. The easily removed cover is made of sheet-type fabric that you wash just as you would bedsheets. To make the bed you simply shake out the duvet and lay it over the bed. You also can use a duvet cover over an ordinary comforter for a change of style. (To make your own duvet cover, see pages 106 and 107.)

Futons

Relative newcomers to Western markets, *futons* are tufted cotton mattresses. Traditional futons are made of layers of cotton batting encased in unbleached muslin or heavier mattress ticking. The cotton batting packs down with use to form a firm sleeping surface; a well-made futon will pack uniformly, without lumps.

Futons originally were designed to be restuffed with fresh cotton every two or three years. Since this no longer is practical, Western manufacturers often add a thin core of high-density foam to the center of the futon for greater and

longer-lasting resilience. Some deluxe models feature an additional padding layer of rubberized horsehair around the foam core.

You can place a futon directly on the floor, or on a slatted wooden bed platform for more flexible support. Most models can be rolled up for storage or folded on special sofa or chair frames so they can double as seating pieces. You can purchase or sew colorful protective covers to go over the futon.

Pillow talk

Whether you prefer a soft pillow you can sink your head into or a firm, resilient one is a matter of personal taste. Pillows are filled with various materials, and within each material category you usually have a choice of soft, medium, or firm.

• The most expensive pillows are made of *goose* or *duck down*. They're lightweight and have a slippery-soft feel and sink-in comfort.

• *Feather* pillows are cheaper than down, but don't feel as luxurious because of the feathers' quills. Feathers often are mixed with down; the higher the percentage of down, the softer the pillow.

• *Synthetic polyester* fillings make more resilient pillows that are mothproof, mildew-proof and nonallergenic. Some new synthetics simulate the feel of down. They're more expensive than ordinary polyester fillings, but cheaper than genuine down.

• *Latex foam* pillows provide buoyant support. They may be molded in one piece or shredded; molded is preferable, because the shredded pieces can feel lumpy after a while.

Better Homes and Gardens® Books

Would you like to learn more about decorating, remodeling, or maintaining your home's bedrooms? These Better Homes and Gardens® books can help.

Better Homes and Gardens®
NEW DECORATING BOOK
How to translate ideas into workable solutions for every room in your home. Choosing a style, furniture arrangements, windows, walls and ceilings, floors, lighting, and accessories. 433 color photos, 76 how-to illustrations, 432 pages.

Better Homes and Gardens®
DOLLAR-STRETCHING DECORATING
Save on furnishings and decorating costs without sacrificing style or comfort. Filled with easy-to-carry-out ideas, practical suggestions, do-it-yourself projects, and how-to drawings. 160 color photos, 125 how-to illustrations, 192 pages.

Better Homes and Gardens®
COMPLETE GUIDE TO HOME REPAIR,
MAINTENANCE, & IMPROVEMENT
Inside your home, outside your home, your home's systems, basics you should know. Anatomy and step-by-step drawings illustrate components, tools, techniques, and finishes. 515 how-to techniques; 75 charts; 2,734 illustrations; 552 pages.

Better Homes and Gardens®
STEP-BY-STEP BUILDING SERIES
A series of do-it-yourself building books that provides step-by-step illustrations and how-to information for starting and finishing many common construction projects and repair jobs around your house. More than 90 projects and 1,200 illustrations in this series of six 96-page books:
STEP-BY-STEP BASIC PLUMBING
STEP-BY-STEP BASIC WIRING
STEP-BY-STEP BASIC CARPENTRY
STEP-BY-STEP HOUSEHOLD REPAIRS
STEP-BY-STEP MASONRY & CONCRETE
STEP-BY-STEP CABINETS & SHELVES

ACKNOWLEDGMENTS

Other Sources of Information

Many professional associations will provide lists of their members to interested consumers; many special-interest associations and manufacturers publish catalogs, style books, and product brochures that are available upon request.

American Society of Interior Designers (ASID)
730 Fifth Avenue
New York, NY 10019

Federal Trade Commission, Bureau of Consumer Protection
Washington, DC 20580

Fieldcrest Mills, Inc.
Publicity Department
60 West 40th Street
New York, NY 10018

Furniture Industry Consumer Advisory Panel (FICAP)
P.O. Box 951
High Point, NC 27261

National Association of Bedding Manufacturers (NABM)
1235 Jefferson Davis Highway
Arlington, VA 22202

National Association of Furniture Manufacturers (NAFM)
8401 Connecticut Avenue
Washington, DC 20015

St. Regis Forest Products
1019 Pacific Avenue
Tacoma, WA 98401

U.S. Plywood
Division of Champion International
777 Third Avenue
New York, NY 10017

Waterbed Manufacturers Assocation
1411 Olympic Boulevard
Los Angeles, CA 90015

Architects and Designers

The following is a listing by page of the interior designers, architects, and project designers whose work appears in this book.

Cover:
David Haupert
Pages 6-7
Pam Sawyer
Pages 8-9
Ast-Daglenen
Pages 10-11
Robert E. Dittmer
Pages 12-13
Pamela Hughes & Company
Pages 14-15
Milton Botterill,
Agars Studio
Pages 16-17
Sam Anthony Cardella
Pages 18-19
David Haupert
Pages 20-21
Larry Boeder
Pages 22-23
Marthe Jocelyn
Pages 24-25
Fran Lechtrecker
Pages 26-27
Ristomatti Ratia
Pages 28-29
Charles Damga
Pages 32-37
Stephen Mead Associates
Pages 70-71
Taylor Siegmeister Associates
Page 72
Sharon Sawyer
Page 73
Pat MacNamara
Pages 74-75
Pamela Hughes, The H.Chambers Company

Page 77
Adek and Drois; Apfelbaum
Pages 78-79
Cherry Brown
Pages 80-81
Glenn Gregg, A.I.A.
Pages 82-83
Gayle Bird
Pages 84-85
Perez Associates, Inc.
Pages 86-87
Bob and Lynne Grogger
Page 105
Virginia Frankel
Pages 106-107
Kate Wharton, Now and Then
Page 108
Suzy Taylor, A.S.I.D.
Page 110
Sue Parr
Page 116
Janet Pierri, A.S.I.D.
Page 117
Barbara Treiman, A.S.I.D.
Pages 118-119
Nancy West, A.S.I.D., West Interiors
Pages 120-121
Jim and Margot Ladwig
Pages 122-123
Ron W. Sorenson
Pages 124-125
Gary Hovda
Pages 126-127
Carver/Karofsky Interiors, Suzanne G. Lipsky, Architect
Pages 128-129
Jennifer Barker and John Armstrong
Pages 130-131
Furniture and Things
Pages 132-133
Donald Singer
Pages 134-135
Kevin Walz
Pages 136-137
David Ashe; Suzy Taylor, A.S.I.D.
Pages 140-141
Lenore Lucey
Pages 142-143
Stephen Mead Associates

Photographers and Illustrators

We extend our thanks to the following photographers and illustrators, whose creative talents and technical skills contributed much to this book.

Ernest Braun
Ross Chapple
George de Gennaro
Mike Dieter
Nanci Doonan
Peter M. Fine
Hedrich-Blessing
Hellman Design Associates, Inc.
Bill Helms
Thomas Hooper
William N. Hopkins
Bill Hopkins, Jr.
Fred Lyon
Maris/Semel
Frank Lotz Miller
Carson Ode
Bradley Olman
Tim Street-Porter
Jessie Walker

Associations and Companies

Our appreciation goes to the following associations and companies for providing information and materials for this book.

Baby Korner
Better Sleep Council
Carolina Mirror Corporation
Childcraft Juvenile Furniture
Dan River
Kleinsleep™ stores of Greater New York
Laura Ashley
Levolor Lorentzen, Inc.
National Association of Mirror Manufacturers
William Kent Schoenfisch, Inc.
Sealy, Inc.
Toledo Mirror
Waterbed Manufacturers Association
WestPoint Pepperell
Wicker Works
Workbench

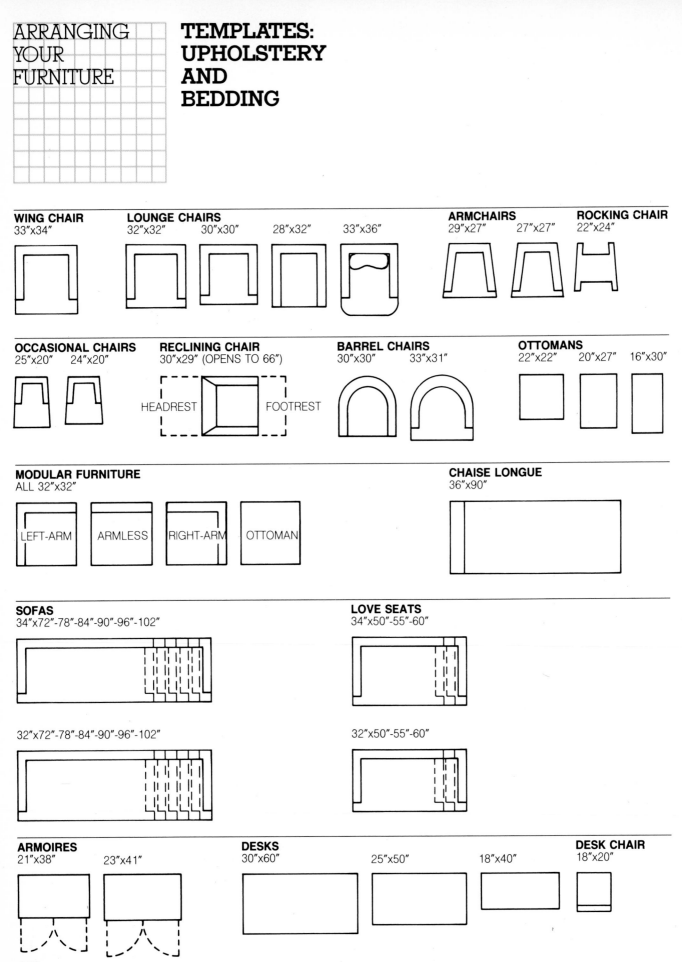

WING CHAIR
33"x34"

LOUNGE CHAIRS
32"x32"   30"x30"   28"x32"   33"x36"

ARMCHAIRS
29"x27"   27"x27"

ROCKING CHAIR
22"x24"

OCCASIONAL CHAIRS
25"x20"   24"x20"

RECLINING CHAIR
30"x29" (OPENS TO 66")

HEADREST   FOOTREST

BARREL CHAIRS
30"x30"   33"x31"

OTTOMANS
22"x22"   20"x27"   16"x30"

MODULAR FURNITURE
ALL 32"x32"

LEFT-ARM   ARMLESS   RIGHT-ARM   OTTOMAN

CHAISE LONGUE
36"x90"

SOFAS
34"x72"-78"-84"-90"-96"-102"

32"x72"-78"-84"-90"-96"-102"

LOVE SEATS
34"x50"-55"-60"

32"x50"-55"-60"

ARMOIRES
21"x38"   23"x41"

DESKS
30"x60"   25"x50"   18"x40"

DESK CHAIR
18"x20"

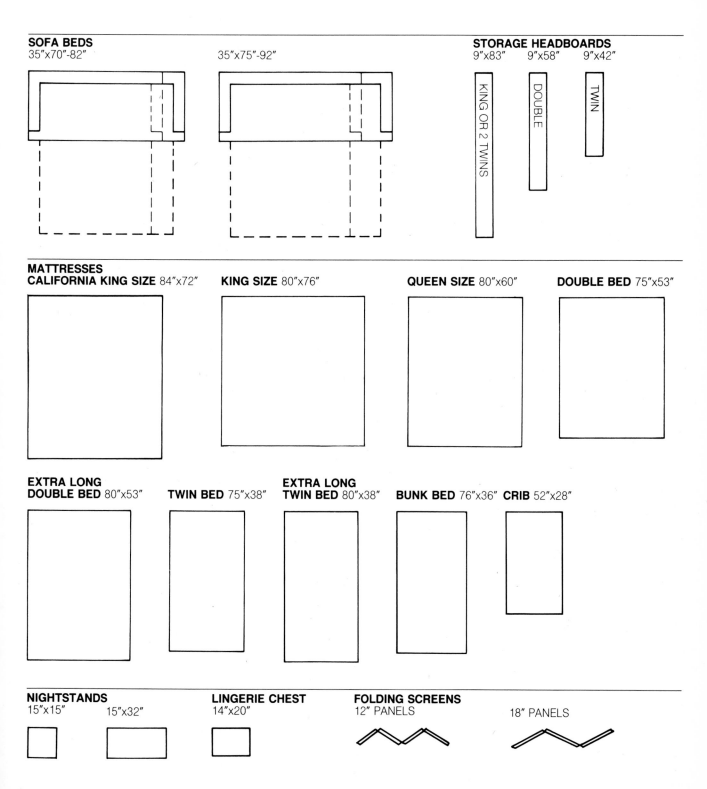

SOFA BEDS
35"x70"-82"

35"x75"-92"

STORAGE HEADBOARDS
9"x83"   9"x58"   9"x42"

KING OR 2 TWINS

DOUBLE

TWIN

MATTRESSES
CALIFORNIA KING SIZE 84"x72"

KING SIZE 80"x76"

QUEEN SIZE 80"x60"

DOUBLE BED 75"x53"

EXTRA LONG
DOUBLE BED 80"x53"

TWIN BED 75"x38"

EXTRA LONG
TWIN BED 80"x38"

BUNK BED 76"x36"   **CRIB** 52"x28"

NIGHTSTANDS
15"x15"   15"x32"

LINGERIE CHEST
14"x20"

FOLDING SCREENS
12" PANELS

18" PANELS

Page numbers in *italics* refer to photographs or illustrations.

A-B

Adding on, *66-67*
  master bedroom, *52-53*
Apartments, efficiency, strategies for, *74-75*
Artwork
  modern, *24*
  traditional scheme, *20-21*
Attic, opened, as play loft, *77*
Attic bedroom, storage system in, *46*
Baths
  bed/bath combination, *82-83*
  in floor-plan alterations, *44, 45, 48-51*
  for children, *65*
Battings, quilt, 109
Bearing versus nonbearing walls, 88
Bedcoverings, *153*
  child's room, *10-11*
  coverlets, making, *112-113*
  quilts, *108-109*
  duvets and duvet covers, *10-11*, 154
  making, *106-107*
  spreads, fitted, making, *110-111*
  style and, *21-23*
Bed curtains, making, *114-115*
Bedrooms
  adding on, *66-67*
    master bedroom, *52-53*
  amenities, *8-9*, 118-131
    fireplaces, *39, 84*, 120, *121, 127*
    guest quarters, *14-15, 130-131*
    lighting, creative, *122-123*
    master wing, *126-127*
    sight-and-sound equipment, setting for, *124-125*

Bedrooms *(contd.)*
  view, enhancement of, *118-119*
  wall removal, open plan from, *128-129*
  bed location, *54-55*
    in master bedroom, *40-41*
  children's. *See* Children's rooms
  color in. *See* Color, use of remodeling case studies
    master bedrooms, *48-51*
    secondary bedrooms, *62-65*
  storage considerations. *See* Storage
  strategies, 70-87
    bed/bath combination, *82-83*
    bunk beds, *78*, 79
    closets, beds in, *72-73*
    for efficiency apartment, *74-75*
    lofts as, *72, 76-77*
    mother-in-law suite, *86-87*
    for small room, *70-71*
    See also Master bedroom, planning
  for wheelchair user, *68-69*
  See also Building projects; Furnishings, purchased; Sewing projects; Style
Beds
  bunk beds, *78*, 79
    project, *138-139*
  in closets, *72-73*
  and color schemes, *32-37*
  cribs, 56
    with chest, *57*
    project, *132-133*
  four-poster, *20-21*
  headboards for, *134-135, 144, 145*

Beds *(contd.)*
  bedding stored in, *19*
  half-moon, *28*
  island, building, *134-135*
  ladder-access, *58*
  locating, *54-55*
    in master bedroom, *40-41*
  loft, *11, 72, 76*
    building, *98-99*
  Murphy, 62, *73*
    project, *136-137*
  painted wood, *22-23*
  pine, antique, *7, 26-27*
  platform, *28-29, 71*
    carpeted, in guest room, *131*
    drawers under, *18-19*
    lighting, *122*
    project, *140-141*
  sizes, 6, 40
  sleigh, antique, *12-13*
  as sofas, *14-15, 74-75*
  space considerations, 6, *7, 16-17, 70-71*
  trundle style, *59, 150-151*
  water beds, *148-149*
    project, *142-143*
  for wheelchair user, *68*, 69
Bedskirts, *11, 111*
  making, 110
Bedspreads, fitted, making, *110-111*
Bench, built-in, *70*
Blankets, 153
Blinds, mini-slat, *21, 33, 120-121*
Bolster pillows, *110*
  sewing, 104
Bookcase headboard, island bed with, *134-135*
Bookcases, *16*
  platform bed with, *140*
Boxes, electrical, installing, *95*
Box springs, 147
Breakfast table, *22-23*
Building projects, 88-103, 132-143
  bunk bed, *138-139*
  closet, *90-91*

Building projects *(contd.)*
  crib, *132-133*
  electrical work, *94-95*
  island bed, *134-135*
  lavatory installation, *92-93*
  mirror installation, *96-97*
  Murphy bed, *136-137*
  noise control, *100-101*
  platform bed, *140-141*
  security improvement, *102-103*
  sleeping loft, *98-99*
  vanities
    cabinet, 93
    electricity, *94-95*
  wall removal, 88, *89*
  water bed, *142-143*
Bunk beds, *78*, 79
  project, *138-139*

C-E

Cabinets, vanity, 93
Cane-seated chair, *21*
Canopy, making, 115
Carpet on beds
  headboard, *134-135*
  sleeping platform, *131*
Casual styling, *22-23*
Chairs
  pine, *27*
  for wheelchair user, *69*
  wicker, *25*
  wooden, cane-seated, *21*
Children's rooms, *10-11, 58-59*
  alternate plans, *54-55, 62-65*
  bath guidelines, 65
  bunk beds, *78, 79, 138-139*

Children's rooms *(contd.)*
 lofts, *11, 72, 76, 77*
 nurseries, furnishings for,
  56-57
  build-it-yourself crib,
   132-133
 storage, *11,* 19, *56-57, 60,*
  61, *79*
  height chart, 61
 wing addition, *66-67*
Chinese rug, *24-25*
Closets
 beds in, *72-73*
 building, *90-91*
 clothes. *See* Clothes storage
Clothes storage, 19
 master bedrooms, *46-47*
 secondary bedrooms, *60-61*
 sleeping loft with, *72*
Color, use of, *30*
 casual scheme, *22-23*
 color schemes
  dark, *36-37*
  neutral, *32-33*
  warm, *34-35*
 color wheel, *31*
 master wing, tying together,
  126-127
 modern scheme, *28-29*
 traditional scheme, *20-21*
Comforters, 153
 duvets, 154
  making, *106-107*
 quilts, *22-23*
  making, *108-109*
 in traditional scheme, *21*
Complementary colors, 31
Convertible sofas, 74
Cornice, making, *116*
Country styling, *26-27*
Coverlets, making, *112-113*
 quilts, *108-109*
Cradle, rocking, *57*
Cribs, 56
 build-it-yourself, *132-133*
 with chest, *57*
Curtains, making
 bed, *114-115*
 shirred, *117*
Dado, color schemes with,
 32-37
Dark color schemes, *36-37*
Decorating styles. *See* Style

Den/guest rooms, *14-15,*
 130-131
Desks
 children's rooms, *58, 59,*
  138-139
 master bedroom, *80-81*
Disabled person, bedroom for,
 68-69
Dividers in children's rooms,
 58, 59
Doilies, framed, and color
 schemes, *32-37*
Doors
 closet, installing, *91*
 noise control, *100,* 101
Draperies, pleated, making,
 116, 116-117
Drawers
 construction, signs of quality
  in, 151
 under platform bed, *18-19*
Dresser, child's, *56*
Dressing areas in master
 bedroom, *46*
 floor-plan alterations and,
  44, 45, 48-50
Dressing table/vanity, *126*
Drywall, use of, 90, *91*
Duck decoy, *26*
Duvets and duvet covers,
 10-11, 154
 making, *106-107*
Eclectic stylic, *12-13, 24-25*
Efficiency apartments,
 strategies for, *74-75*
Electrical receptacles, 43
Electrical work, *94-95*
Electric blankets, 153

F-O

Fabric samples, *32, 34, 36*
Faucet set, installing, *92*
Fire extinguishers, 103
Fireplaces, *39,* 120, *121, 127*
 in master suite, *84*

Flange-edged pillows, 104,
 105
Flocked blankets, 153
Foam mattresses, 147
Four-poster bed, *20-21*
Framing of closet, *90*
Furnishings, purchased,
 144-154
 headboards, 144, *145*
 mattresses, *146-147*
 soft goods, *152-153,*
  153-154
 storage, *150-151*
 water beds, *148-149*
Furniture arrangement
 master bedroom, *40-41*
 templates for, *156-157*
Futons, 154
"Gladys Goose" lamps, *56-57*
Ground fault circuit interrupter
 (GFCI), wiring, *95*
Guest rooms, *14-15, 130-131*
 alternate plans, *54-55, 62-63*
 closets, 61
Headboards, 144, *145*
 bedding stored in, *19*
 half-moon, *28*
 island bed with, *134-135*
Informal styling, *22-23*
Innerspring mattresses, 147
 spring configurations, *146*
Island bed, *134-135*
Joint compound, use of, *91*
Knife-edged pillows, 104, *111*
Lamps
 around bed, *12, 23, 33,*
  42-43
 "Gladys Goose," 56-57
Lavatory, installing, *92-93*
Lighting
 bed, lamps around, *12, 23,*
  33, 42-43
 "Gladys Goose" lamps,
  56-57
 special effects, *122-123*
 for vanity, 94
Living room, Murphy bed in,
 73
Load-bearing versus
 nonbearing walls, 88
Lofts, *11, 76-77*
 building, *98-99*
 in closet, *72*

Log Cabin quilt, *108,* 109
Love seat near fireplace, *121*
Master bedroom, planning,
 38-53
 adding on, *52-53*
 bed, locating, *40-41*
 bed/bath combination,
  82-83
 bedside items, *42-43*
 case studies in remodeling,
  48-51
 expansion, *80-81*
 extra features, alterations
  for, *44-45*
 storage, clothes, *46-47*
 super-suite, *84-85*
 templates, *156-157*
 wall removal, *80-81, 88,*
  128-129
 See also Bedrooms:
  amenities
Master wing, *126-127*
Mattress covers, making,
 110-111
Mattresses, *146-147*
 futons, 154
 sizes, *146-147*
 springs, *146,* 147
 water bed, 148
Mini-slat blinds, *21, 33,*
 120-121
Mirrors, installing, *96-97*
Mirror tiles, *97*
Modern styling, *28-29*
Modular storage units,
 150-151
Mother-in-law suites, *86-87*
Murphy beds, 62, *73*
 project, *136-137*
Neutral color schemes, *32-33*
Noise control, *100-101*
Nonbearing versus load-
 bearing walls, 88
Nurseries, furnishings for,
 56-57
 build-it-yourself crib,
  132-133
Open-plan bedrooms, *128-129*

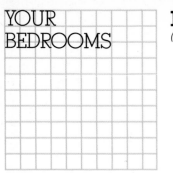
P-S

Patchwork quilts, making, *108-109*
Pillowcase, sewing, 104
Pillow fillings, 104
Pillow quilting, *109*
Pillows, *23, 105*
  kinds, 154
  making, 104
  to match bedspreads, *110-111*
  for sofa beds, *74, 75*
Platform beds, *28-29, 71*
  carpeted, in guest room *131*
  drawers under, *18-19*
  lighting, *122*
  project, *140-141*
Projects. *See* Building projects; Sewing projects
Quilted coverlet, making, *112-113*
Quilts
  in casual scheme, *22-23*
  making, *108-109*
Rag rug, *26-27*
Reading lamps, *23*
Reading room/bedroom, *16-17*
Rugs
  Chinese, *24-25*
  geometric, *12-13*
  rag, *26-27*
Security, improving, *102-103*
Sewing projects, 104-117
  bed curtains, *114-115*
  bedskirt, 110, *111*
  canopy, 115
  coverlets, *112-113*
    quilts, *108-109*
  duvets and duvet covers, *106-107*
  pillows and pillow shams, 104, *105*
  tablecloth, *117*
  window treatments, *116-117*

Sheets
  bed curtains from, *114-115*
  coverlet from, *112-113*
  fabric quality, 153
  tablecloth from, *117*
  yardage from, 112
Shelves
  beside bed, *18*
  bookcases, *16*
    headboard, *134-135*
    platform bed with, *140*
  children's room, *79*
  closet, guidelines for, *47*
Shirred curtains, making, *117*
Side curtains, making, *114-115*
Sink, installing, *92-93*
Sitting room in master wing, *127*
Skylights, areas with
  divided children's room, *58*
  loft, *77*
  solarium, *85*
  storage core of open plan, *128*
Sleeping lofts, *11, 76*
  building, *98-99*
  in closet, *72*
Sleep sofas, 74
Sleigh bed, antique, *12-13*
Smoke detectors, 103
Sofas, beds as, *14-15, 74-75*
Soft goods, *152-153,* 153-154
  See also Bedcoverings
Solarium, *85*
Sound control, *100-101*
Sound transmission class (STC), 100
Springs, mattress, *146,* 147
Stained-glass window panel, *7*
Stereo and video equipment, setting for, *124-125*

Storage, *18-19, 150-151*
  bookcases, *16*
    headboard, *134-135*
    platform bed with, *140*
  children's rooms, *11,* 19, *56-57, 60,* 61, *79*
  clothes, 19
    master bedrooms, *46-47*
    secondary bedrooms, *60-61*
    sleeping loft combined with, *72*
  division of areas with, *128-129*
  and lighting effects, *123*
  sight-and-sound setting, *124-125*
  small bedroom, *70, 71*
Study in master bedroom, *80-81*
Style, 20-29
  casual, *22-23*
  country, *26-27*
  eclectic, *12-13, 24-25*
  modern, *28-29*
  traditional, *20-21*
Super-suites, *84-85*

T-W

Tablecloth, round, making, *117*
Tables
  breakfast, *22-23*
  Murphy bed with, *136*
  Parsons, as desk/night table, *130*
  pine, *27*
  skirted, *25*
Television, setting for, *124-125*
Templates for furniture arrangement, *156-157*
Texture, use of, *32-33*
Thermal blankets, 153
Toy chest, *56-57*
Traditional styling, *20-21*
Trundle-style beds, *59, 150-151*

Vanities
  cabinets, 93
  and dressing table, *126*
  electricity for, *94-95*
  lavatories, installing, *92-93*
Ventilation of bed/bath suite, 82
Walk-in closets, storage maximization in, *47*
Walls
  load-bearing versus nonbearing, 88
  mirrors on, *96-97*
  noise-insulation systems, *100-101*
  removal, 88, *89*
  for master bedroom, *80-81, 88, 128-129*
Warm color schemes, *34-35*
Water beds, *142-143, 148-149*
Wheelchair user, bedroom for, *68-69*
Wicker furniture, *25*
Windows and noise control, 101
Window treatments
  sewing projects, *116-117*
  space-saving, *7*
  style and
    casual, *22*
    modern, *29*
    traditional, *21*
  for view enhancement, 118
Wiring, *94-95*
Wool blankets, 153

Have BETTER HOMES AND
GARDENS® magazine
delivered to your door.
For information, write to:
MR. ROBERT AUSTIN
P.O. BOX 4536
DES MOINES, IA 50336